AF372106

Kiki Kogelnik

Fly Me to the Moon

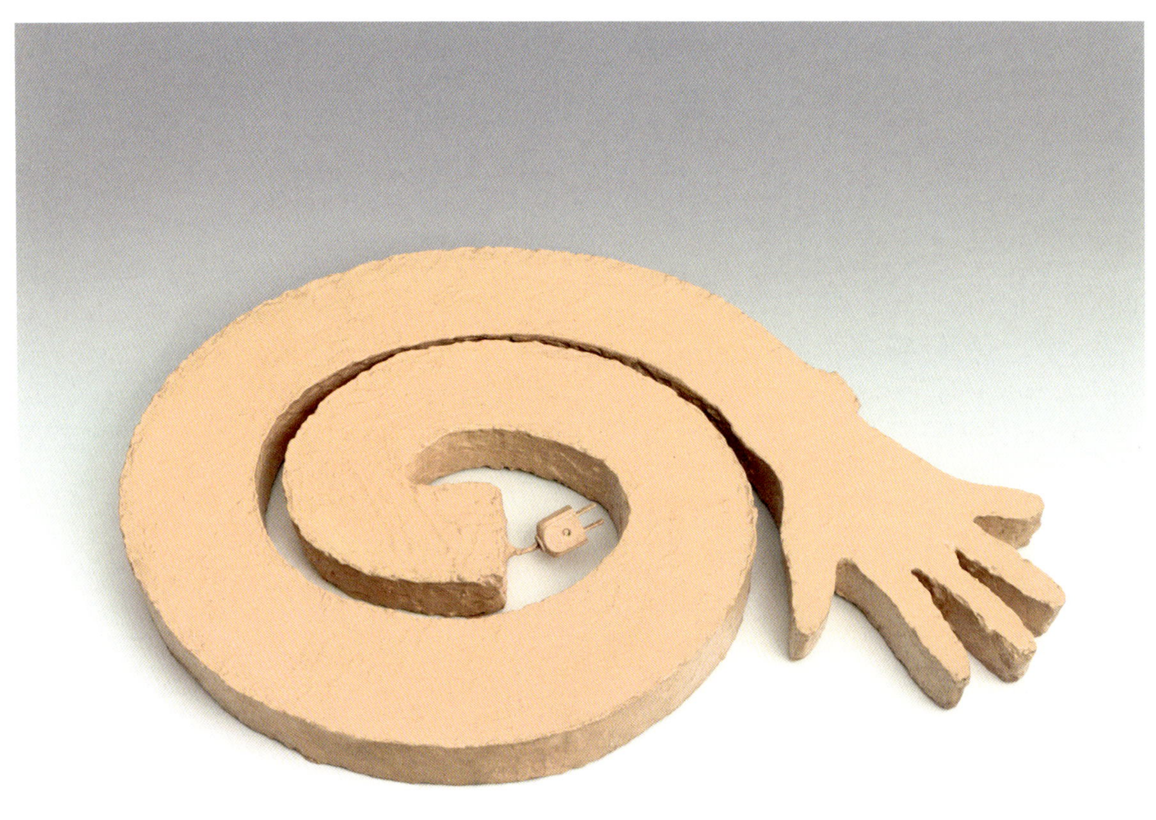

Plug-in Hand, c. 1967
Acrylic on polyurethane and paper mache
67.5 × 43.6 × 5 cm

Foreword

Modern Art Oxford is honoured to present the first solo exhibition in the UK by the late Austrian artist, Kiki Kogelnik (1935 – 97). Surprisingly unknown outside of her homeland, Kogelnik is widely considered to be the most important Austrian artist of her generation associated with Pop art, an association that she contested during her lifetime.

Born in Bleiburg in Southern Austria, Kogelnik studied at the Vienna Academy of Fine Art in the mid 1950s, where her practice focused on abstract painting. In 1961, Kogelnik moved to New York, where she joined a close-knit group of artists that included Jasper Johns, Roy Lichtenstein, Joan Mitchell, Claes Oldenburg, Robert Rauschenberg, Larry Rivers, Andy Warhol and Tom Wesselmann. It was during this time that her work began to show synergies with Pop art in her energetic and playful use of synthetic materials, such as plastic and vinyl, her bright exuberant colours and dynamic kaleidoscopic compositions.

During the early 1960s, Kogelnik began to use life-size cut-out paper stencils of her friends to produce her paintings. In 1965 these prototype cut-outs became vinyl hangings, presented on the same clothing racks that she saw pushed down the streets in the vicinity of her studio in New York's Garment District. It is this exciting period of Kogelnik's production in the 1960s and early 1970s, characterised by an engagement with contemporary events such as the space race, the Cold War, technological innovation and feminism that is the focus of the exhibition at Modern Art Oxford.

I would like to take this opportunity to express our most sincere thanks to Mono Schwarz-Kogelnik and the staff at the Kiki Kogelnik Foundation, Dr George Schwarz, and the Simone Subal Gallery in New York, whose collective advice, support and generosity has made this important show possible. I would like to thank the Modern Art Oxford team, especially my colleagues Ciara Moloney, who has curated this exhibition with scholarship and sensitivity, Paul Teigh, who played a key role in the design and realisation of the show and Jonathan Weston, for his work on this publication. Our thanks are also due to Marco

Livingstone for his initial guidance in researching and developing the exhibition, and to Dr Caoimhín Mac Giolla Léith of University College Dublin for his insightful contribution to this catalogue.

This is a long overdue exhibition of an artist who has been overlooked for decades. It is our intention, in bringing this major figure to a wider national and international audience, that she will now secure a fitting place in the history of twentieth-century art.

Paul Hobson

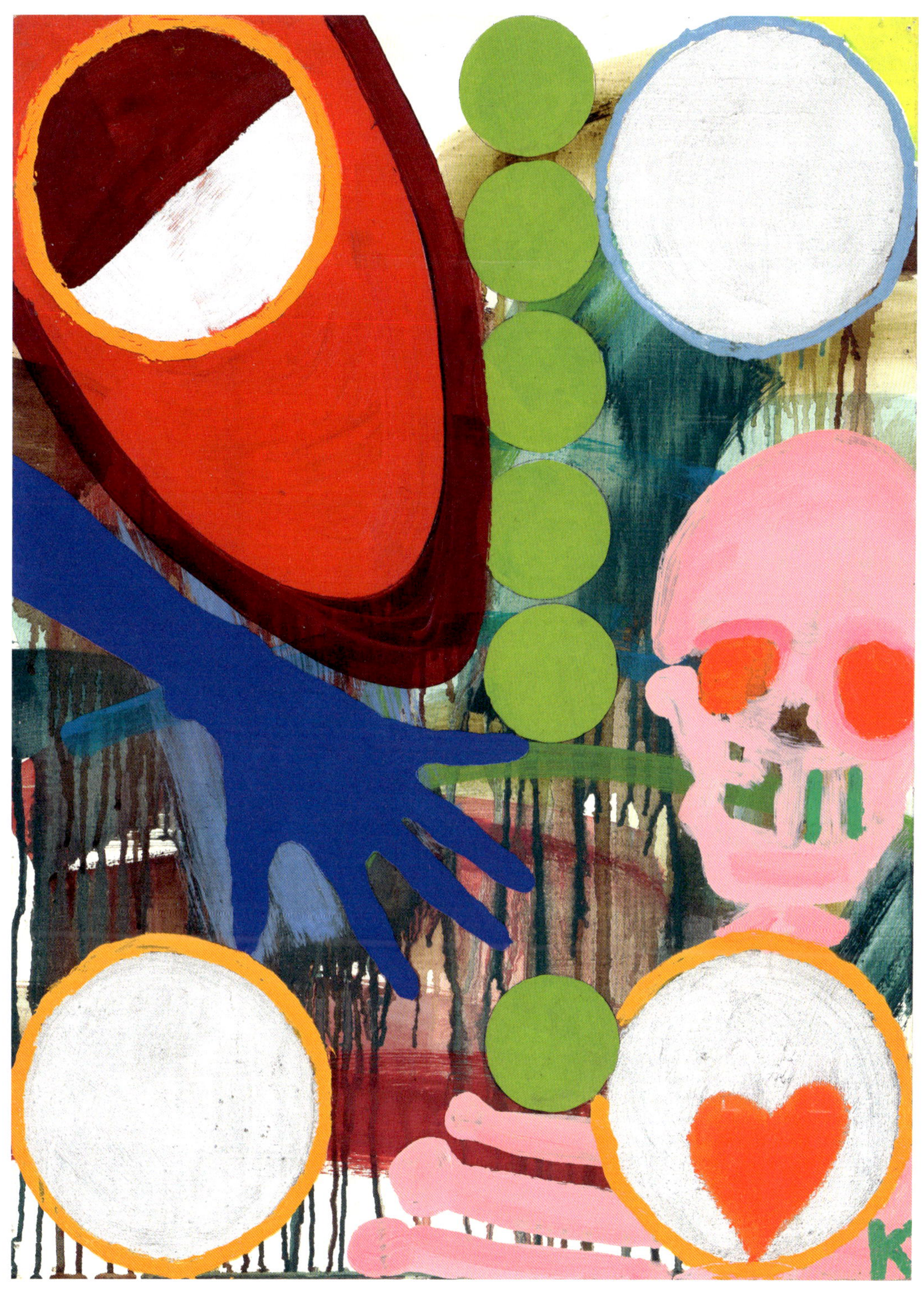

Untitled (Skull), 1960
Oil on panel
60 × 44.5 cm

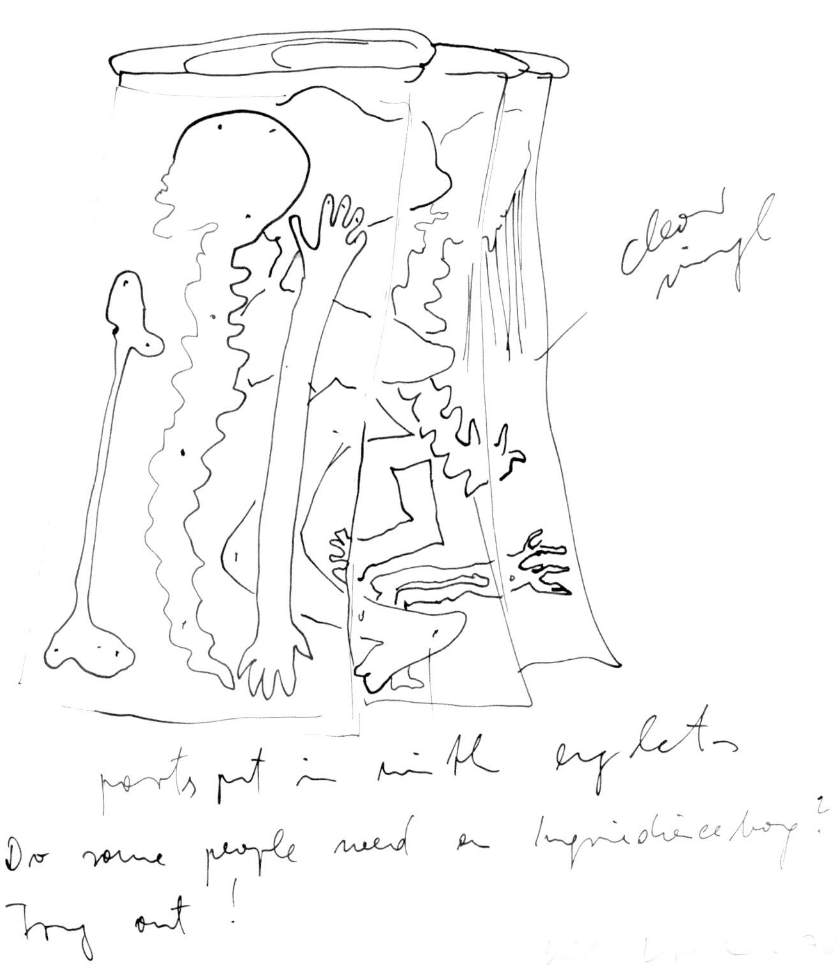

Ingredients Bags, 1970
India ink on paper
35.5 × 27.8 cm

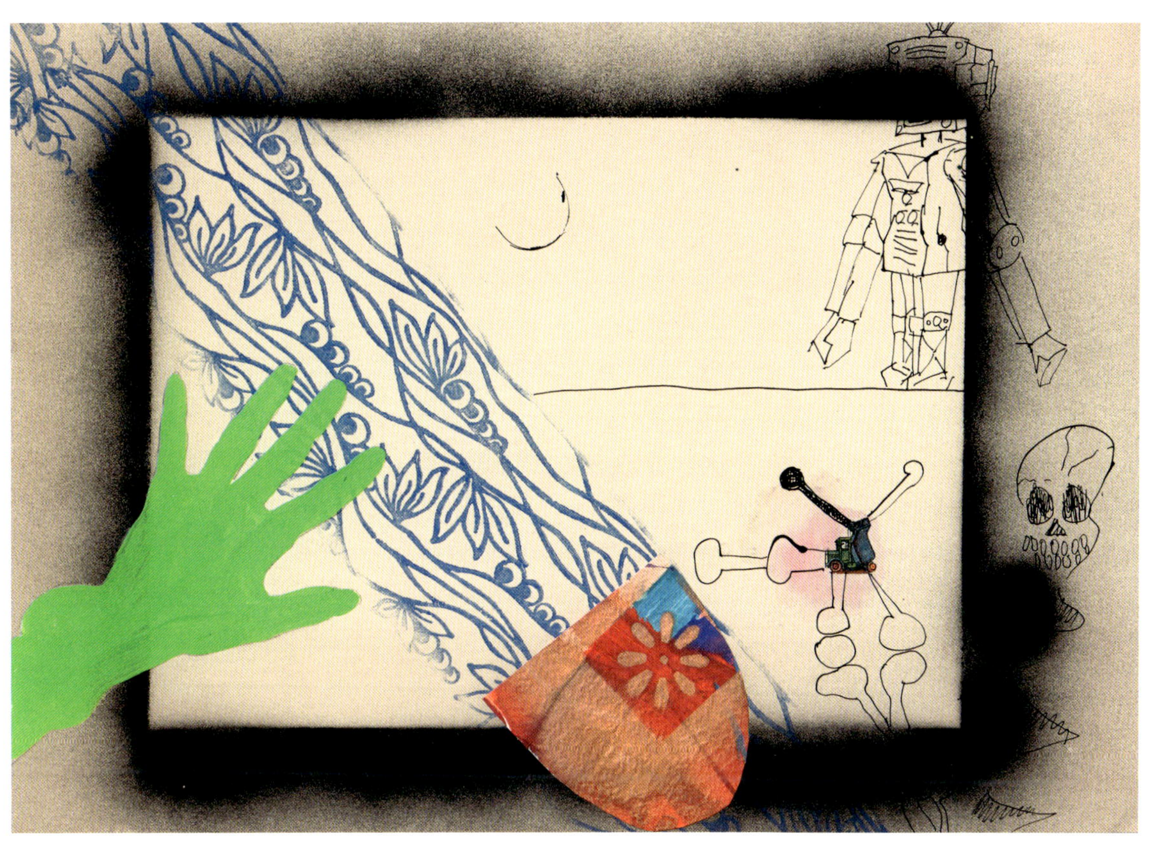

Untitled (Still life with robot, skull and hand), c.1963
Acrylic, enamel, India ink, ink and collage on paper
43.7 × 63 cm

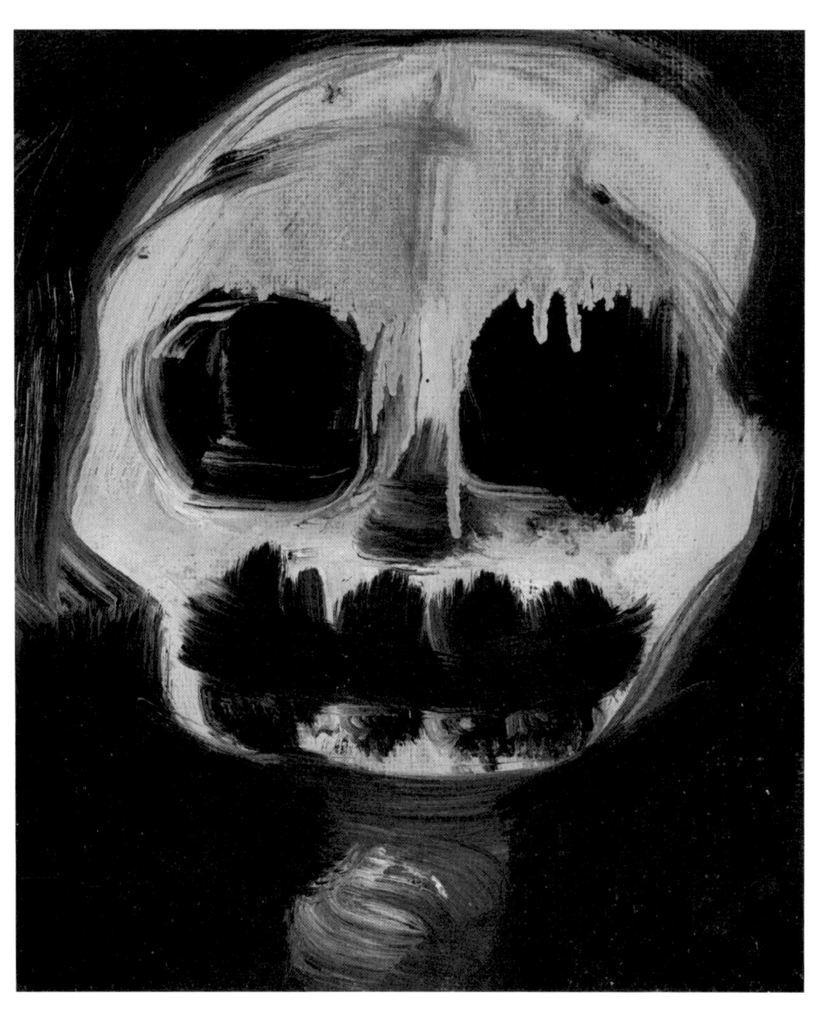

Untitled (Skull), c. 1963
Oil on board
29 × 23.7 cm

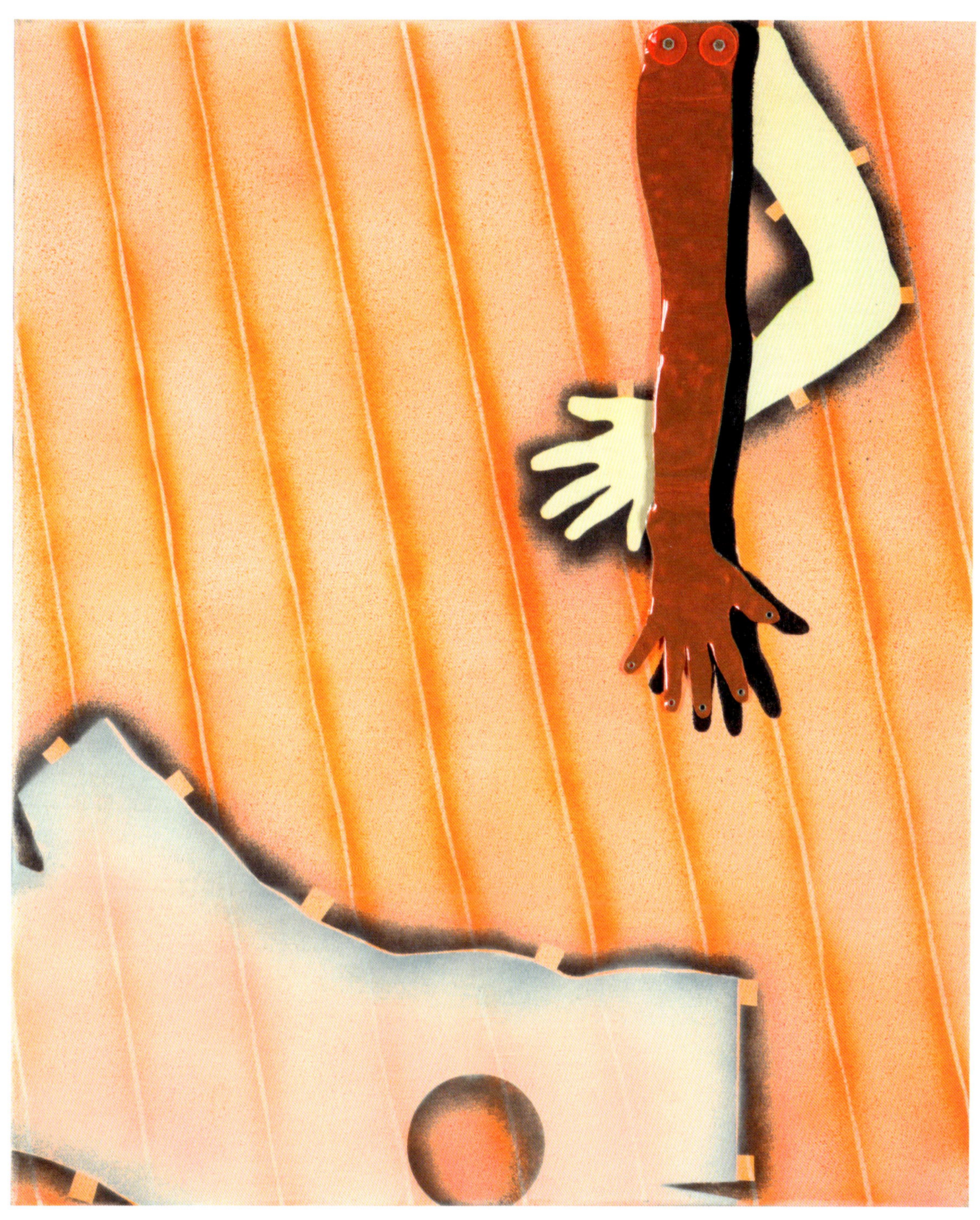

Artificial Hand, 1966
Acrylic with mixed media and metallic foil on canvas
121.1 × 100.6 cm

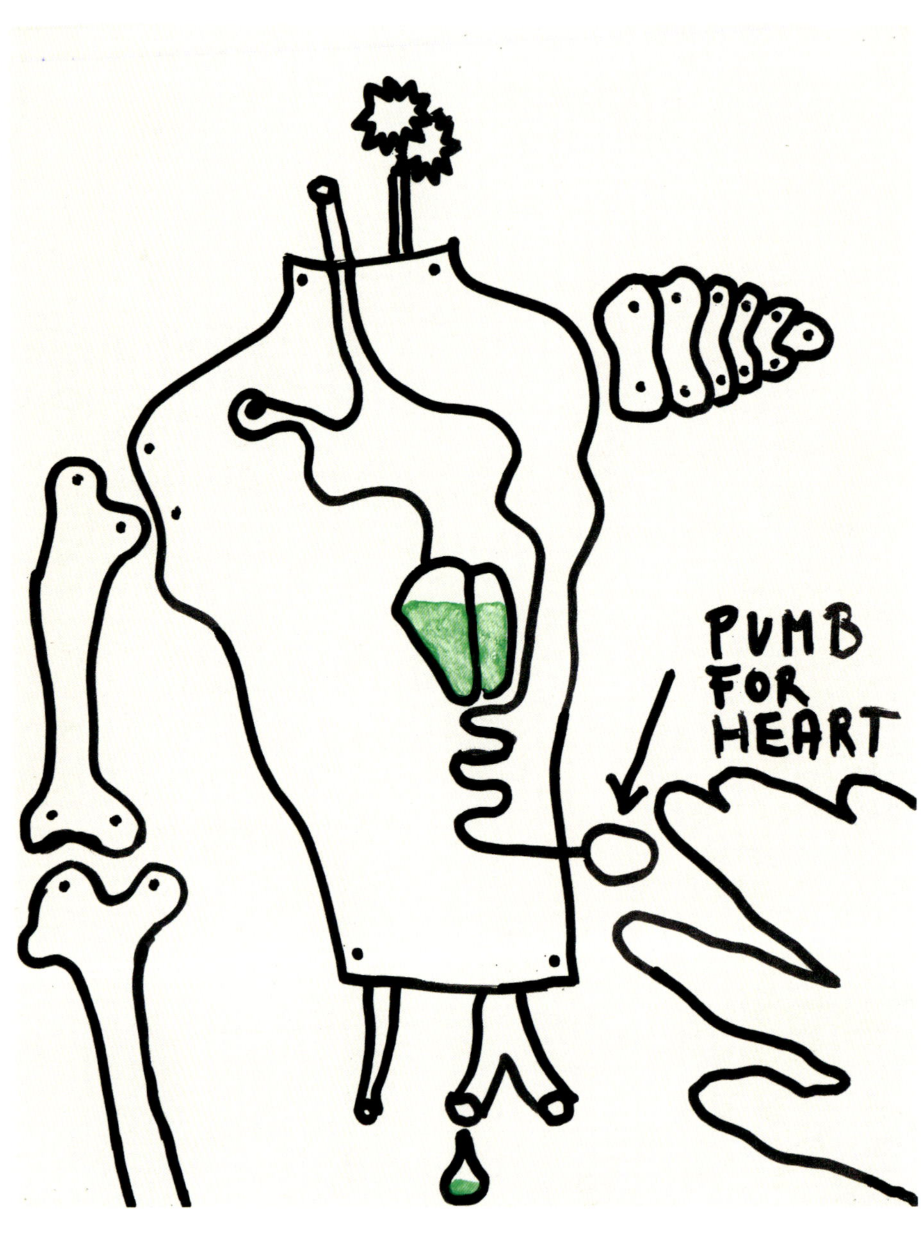

Untitled (Pump for heart), 1965
India ink and acrylic on paper
35.2 × 27.7 cm

Chandelier Hanging, c. 1970
Sheet vinyl with acrylic hanger
79.1 × 46.2 × 46.5 cm

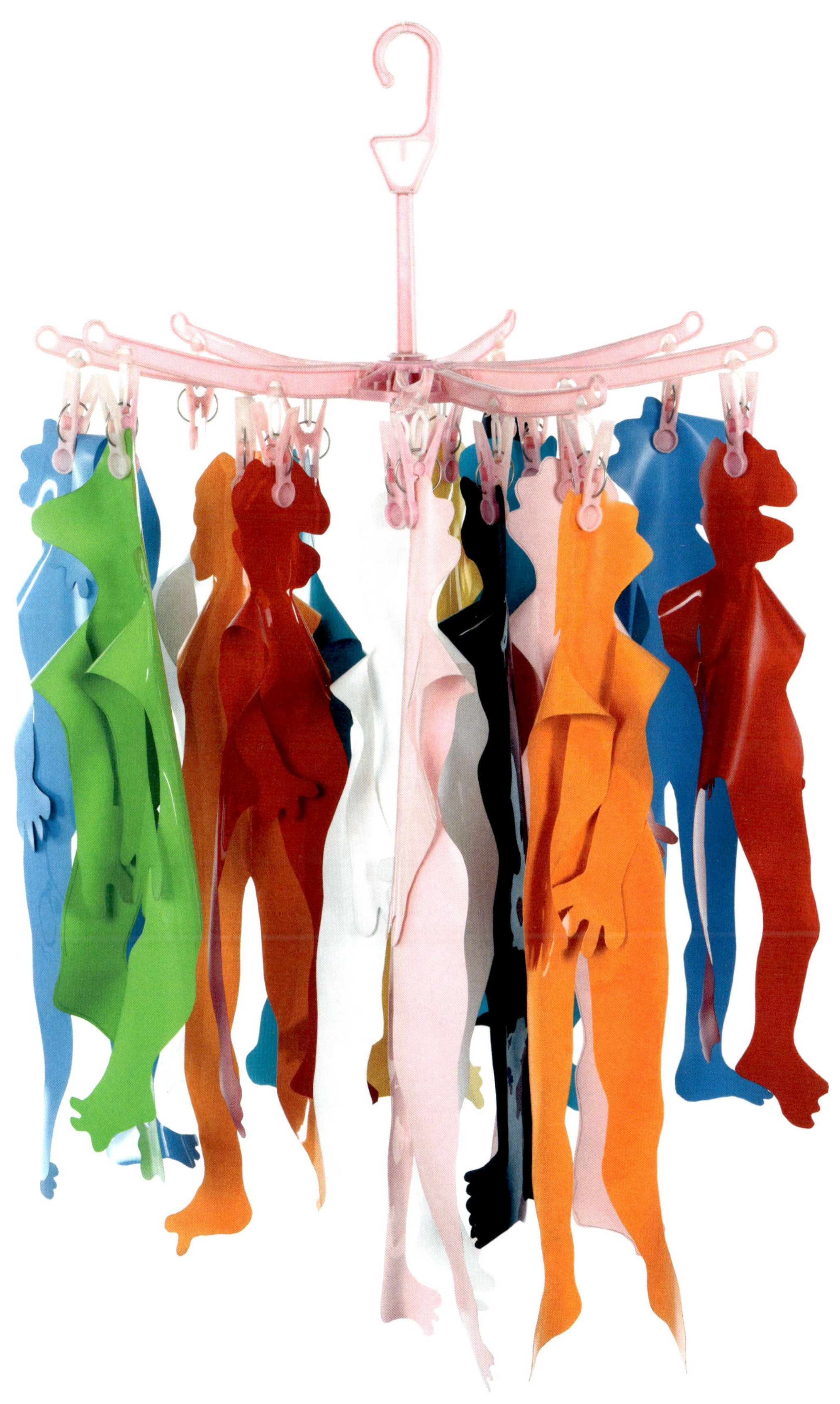

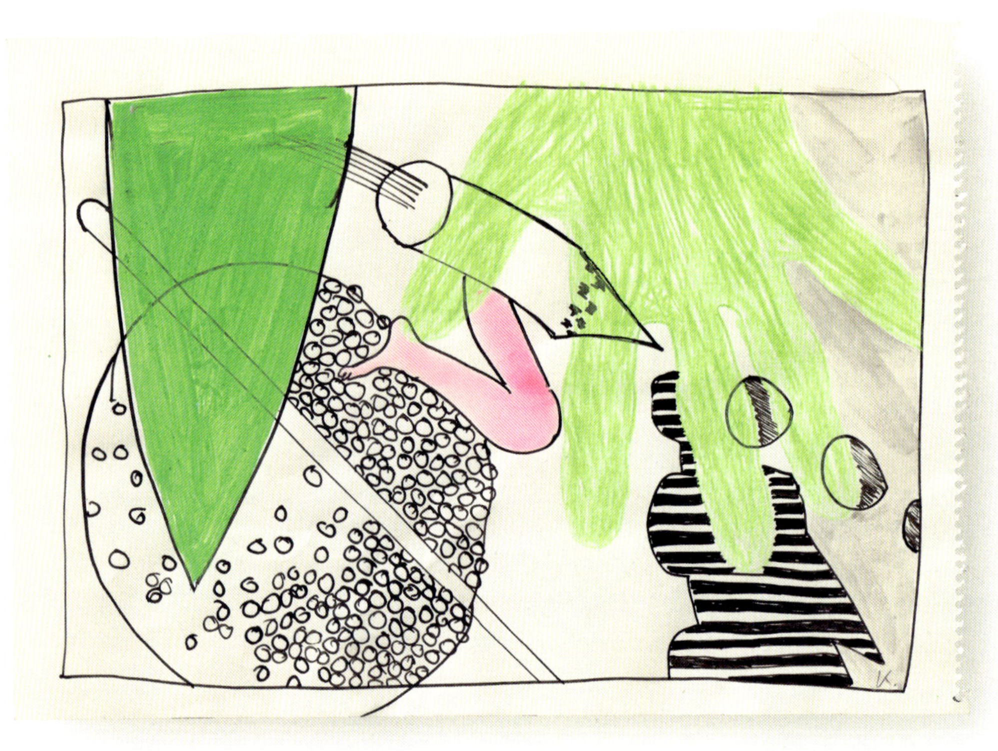

Untitled (Spaceship), c. 1963
Acrylic, India ink and colour pencil on paper
21.3 × 29.4 cm

Love and Rockets

I am chiefly concerned with the representation of an artificial human being in my paintings.[1]

Kiki Kogelnik

In 1886 the French Symbolist writer Auguste Villiers de l'Isle-Adam published an early science-fiction novel, *L'Ève future*, whose eponymous heroine is a misogynist's dream of a compliant female android created by, of all people, a fictionalised Thomas Edison. Such robotic Galateas recur in high art and popular culture throughout the following century, most famously in the form of the demonically seditious femme fatale in Fritz Lang's dystopian classic of German Expressionist cinema, *Metropolis* (1927), partly inspired by De l'Isle-Adam's novel. Yet by 1985 the figure of the machinic human body had somehow accrued enough radical, liberatory potential to function as an emblem of a socialist feminist vision of the future in Donna Haraway's epochal *Cyborg Manifesto* (1991):

> By the late-twentieth century, our time, a mythic time, we are
> all chimeras, theorized and fabricated hybrids of machine and
> organism; in short we are cyborgs… The cyborg is a creature
> in a post-gender world; it has no truck with bi-sexuality, pre-
> Oedipal symbiosis, unalienated labour, or other seductions
> to organic wholeness…[2]

Born in the same year that Haraway published her manifesto, the American singer, songwriter and producer Janelle Monáe released an acclaimed concept album, *The ArchAndroid* (2010), starring her own creation, Cindi Mayweather, as alter ego, muse and messianic icon of what she styled as the 'new other'. Drawing on disparate sources, from the imaginative legacy of Afro-futurism to the regimented inhumanity depicted in Lang's *Metropolis*, Monáe complemented her music by the performance of a cross-dressing, androgynous persona that contrived to be at once de-individuated and charismatic, driven by robotic energy and riven by human eccentricity.

---

[1] Quoted by Angela Stief, 'Attention and Repulsion in Kiki Kogelnik's Paintings from the 1960s' in Florian Waldvogel (ed.), *Kiki Kogelnik: I Have Seen the Future!*, Kunstverein Hamburg/Snoeck, Hamburg and Cologne, 2012, p. 74.

[2] Donna Haraway, 'A Manifesto for Cyborgs: Science, Technology, and Socialist Feminism in the 1980s', *The Haraway Reader*, Routledge, New York and London, 2004, pp. 8–9.

Born and trained in Austria before relocating to New York in 1961 in her mid-20s, Kiki Kogelnik made her own signal contribution to this tradition of futuristic sociocultural speculation, especially during the crucial decade following her arrival in America. She once offered a pithy account of her concerns as an artist: 'I'm involved in the technical beauty of rockets, people flying in space, and people becoming robots'.[3] The image of a two-dimensional, fragmentary, de-differentiated and often (though not always) gender-neutral body, sometimes composed of mechanical as well as organic parts, is a pervasive motif in her work. This motif evolved in particular ways in response to changing times. In the early 1960s, as the primordial dream of unassisted human flight was transformed into realistic expectations of a technologically engineered landing on the surface of the moon, anonymous human silhouettes float or tumble through fields of multicoloured motifs, abstract and figurative, which drift across the shallow pictorial spaces of Kogelnik's paintings like so much interplanetary debris. Yet, if the technological advances of the time allowed humankind to reach for the stars, they also facilitated more earthbound forms of territorial aggression. Kogelnik's 1963 sculpture *Bombs in Love*, a pair of romantically conjoined but undeniably phallic explosive devices – repurposed Second World War ordnance, as it happens, gaily painted and festooned with transparent hearts – was produced around the same time as Stanley Kubrick's *Dr Strangelove or: How I Learned to Stop Worrying and Love the Bomb* (1964). Informed by her exposure to advanced forms of sculpture – the Museum of Modern Art, New York's groundbreaking 1961 exhibition *The Art of Assemblage* surely had a general impact – this work anticipated by several years the popularisation of the countercultural slogan 'Make Love, Not War'. By the mid-1960s, as American military involvement in Vietnam intensified, her paintings' flattened figures become pale, stencilled shades – briskly sprayed on rather than patiently brushed in – augmented by mechanical elements such as cogs, wheels and gears. While the Utopian dream of a beautiful union between human and machine has yet to fade, the cropped bodies, sundered limbs and outstretched hands in these pictures seem in retrospect to be as redolent of constriction, disintegration and supplication as they are of streamlined prosthetic enhancement.

Given how fresh these works look today, it is tempting to view Kogelnik as a prescient harbinger of our current, ostensibly posthuman condition. She was

---

[3] Quoted in Alexandra Hennig, 'Robot Fantasies, or How the Bombs Learned to Love' in Hans-Peter Wipplinger (ed.), *Kiki Kogelnik: Retrospektive/Retrospective*, Kunsthalle Krems, Krems, 2013, p. 39.

certainly not immune to what John Johnston has termed *The Allure of Machinic Life* (2008) in a book that examines the recent development of such techno-human hybridic forms as digital organisms, computer immune systems, artificial protocells, evolutionary robotics and swarm systems.[4] Nevertheless, as philosopher Rosi Braidotti has cautioned, '[from] the modernist fantasy of eroticizing the human-machine interaction, to the postmodernist disenchantment, or at least ironical distance from the technological object, something fundamental shifted'.[5] That something was the traumatic fallout of some of the twentieth century's most catastrophic technological innovations, especially over the course of two World Wars and the subsequent proxy wars fought in Asia during the Cold War period. Yet Kogelnik clung on to that modernist fantasy longer than most. The artist who once stated that 'I would like to have a robot who would say good morning, how beautiful you are, I love you' actually constructed a larger-than-life robot sculpture, *Loverboy* (c. 1965), since lost, from a large plastic sphere and a profusion of muffin trays, pie plates and metal soup cans.[6] The mechanised bodies in her paintings hark back to the idealistic aspirations and oneiric musings of the early-twentieth-century avant garde as much as they anticipate our twenty-first-century moment. They are in a line of succession from Francis Picabia's 'mechanomorphs', a series of mechanical drawings of commonplace industrial objects, presented as portraits of individuals, both specific (the photographer Alfred Stieglitz pictured as a camera), and generic (a spark plug described as a 'young American girl in a state of nudity'). This series was mostly executed in 1915, just as Marcel Duchamp was embarking on the schematic depiction of his Mechanical Bride and Bachelor Machine in the great hybrid drawing-sculpture *The Bride Stripped Bare by Her Bachelors, Even (The Large Glass)* (1915–23). Kogelnik's mid 1960s 'robot drawings' and paintings also recall the technophilic reveries of the progenitors of British Pop, Richard Hamilton and Eduardo Paolozzi, in the 1950s.

It is Kogelnik's association with American Pop art that has received most attention to date. She began in the 1950s as a gestural painter in the Abstract Expressionist / Art Informel mode of the day, epitomised in Austria by artists such as Arnulf Rainer, to whom she was briefly engaged, and she was originally persuaded to move to the US by the Californian Abstract Expressionist painter Sam Francis. In New York, however, she acquired a new circle of friends, which

[4] John Johnston, *The Allure of Machinic Life: Cybernetics, Artificial Life and the New AI*, MIT Press, Cambridge, MA, 2008.

[5] Rosi Braidotti, *The Posthuman*, Polity, Cambridge, 2013, p. 109.

[6] Quoted in Alexandra Hennig, *op.cit.*, p. 39.

included some of the leading lights of the emergent Pop art movement, such as Roy Lichtenstein, Claes Oldenburg and Andy Warhol, though she also retained her links with the Austrian art world. While she was welcomed into this coterie, her work has since suffered the same marginalisation in canonical accounts of the period as that of her female peers. Many of these, as art historian Kalliopi Minioudaki has argued, were subjected to the further indignity of being ignored again during later waves of feminist art-historical rediscovery and retrieval, largely due to a prevailing belief in Pop art's irredeemable masculinism.[7] Typical of this assumption is Martha Rosler's declaration that 'there was no space for women in pop…no room for the voicing of a different, "truly" female subjectivity'.[8] Woman functioned rather as object or icon. That this may have been true in life as in art is suggested by a sardonic remark made by Carolee Schneemann, a studio neighbour of Kogelnik's at one point, who said: 'You really have to have been considered beautiful to be accepted by the male art club, and I called us the "cunt mascots"…'[9] It is only very recently that the subversive subtleties of women artists working within a broadly defined Pop idiom have come to be reassessed in exhibitions such as *POWER UP – Female Pop Art*, a revelatory group show curated by Angela Stief at the Kunsthalle Wien in 2010. Alongside the more or less canonical works of Niki de Saint Phalle and Marisol, that show's roster featured maverick psycho-sexual chronicler Dorothy Iannone and crusading Californian nun Sister Corita, as well as a number of their more obscure contemporaries from both sides of the Atlantic: New Yorker Rosalyn Drexler, Hollywood-born but UK-based Jann Haworth, Belgian Evelyne Axell, Christa Dichgans from Berlin and, of course, the Austrian Kiki Kogelnik.

As the 1960s shaded into the 1970s, Kogelnik registered equally the previous decade's triumphs, failures and transformations. She celebrated the culmination of the space race, when Apollo 11 landed on the moon, by staging a *Moonhappening* in Vienna on 20 July 1969 during which she recorded the moon-walking astronauts' words on silk-screens as soon as they uttered them. But she also provided mordant commentary on unfolding events in the public sphere, from the ongoing war in Vietnam to revelations of corruption in the Nixon administration, in a series of increasingly macabre ink drawings. It is not entirely surprising that the Women's Liberation movement attracted her

[7] Kalliopi Minioudaki, 'Other('s) Pop: Return of the Repressed of Two Discourses' in *POWER UP – Female Pop Art*, Kunsthalle Wien/Dumont, Vienna, 2010, p. 135.

[8] Martha Rosler, 'The Figure of the Artist. The Figure of the Woman,' *Decoys and Disruptions: Selected Writings 1975–2001*, MIT Press in association with ICP, Cambridge, MA and New York, NY, 2004, pp. 99–100.

[9] Quoted in Susanne Längle, 'The Many Faces of Kiki K' in Hans-Peter Wipplinger (ed.), *op.cit.*, p. 28.

attention not through the well-researched arguments of Betty Friedan or the evangelistic journalism of Gloria Steinem but through the violent rhetoric of Valerie Solanas, author of the *S.C.U.M. Manifesto* (1967) and her attempted murder of Andy Warhol on 3 June 1968. Several Kogelnik drawings from 1970 titled 'Woman's Liberation' feature a fiercesome woman in a floppy hat, dark sunglasses, a long trench coat and laced-up boots. In one she wields an automatic weapon in a manner reminiscent of images relating to the 1968 performance *Aktionshose: Genitalpanik* by Kogelnik's compatriot VALIE EXPORT. In another she wields a pair of giant scissors. While this latter image, which recurs in larger paintings, is clearly a reference to Solanas's *S.C.U.M.* (Society for Cutting Up Men) it also signals the significance of scission – of cutting out as well as cutting up – in Kogelnik's practice as a whole.

Although the flat, featureless silhouette had long featured in her work as a symbol of generalised humanity, this figure came into its own in the 'Hangings', a body of work originating in a street action of 1967, but mostly deriving from the everyday sight in New York's Garment District of chromed racks full of clothing draped over metal hangers being wheeled up and down the streets. Kogelnik produced many such assemblages of floppy, life-size silhouettes excised from sheets of brightly coloured vinyl, their cumulative anonymity belying the fact that each of them had been generated by cutting around the prone outline of a friend or acquaintance who had been persuaded to 'pose' for the artist. As various drawings relating to the war in Vietnam attest, the abstraction of flesh-and-blood individuals to racks of lifeless ciphers, apparently left hanging or hung out to dry, acquired a particular resonance as growing numbers of vinyl body bags were being shipped home from South East Asia. More fundamental in the long run, however, are the implications of Kogelnik's consistent renunciation of difference and individuation in her depiction of the human form. This is allied, however paradoxically, with the cultivation of a chameleon-like persona constantly performing for the camera in artfully posed studio shots or choreographed street actions. Relentlessly artificial and highly stylised, the panoply of roles through which she flitted ironically – sassy sex goddess, hard-hatted labourer, scissors-wielding manhater, consort of robots – predate by many years comparable strategies of restless mutation by Cindy Sherman in the 1970s and Madonna in the 1980s, as well as more recent performances of mutant or multiple selves such as that of Janelle Monáe. As curator and writer Florian Waldvogel has argued:

> Kogelnik's abnegated freedom of the individual, as visualised in the image of fragments and machines, is part of a superordinate aesthetic model. This model destroys the definition of the subject laid down by Enlightenment discourse. Man is not autonomous; he is divisible and commonplace.[10]

One might express this in stronger terms still. Of the artists of her era, perhaps only Yayoi Kusama displayed a more instinctive and persistent yearning for the dissolution of the human subject into a surrounding field of objects and surfaces, an all-enveloping cosmos of vibrant matter. In this we may yet find that Kiki Kogelnik was truly prophetic.

Dr Caoimhín Mac Giolla Léith

[10] Florian Waldvogel (ed.), *op.cit.*, p. 43.

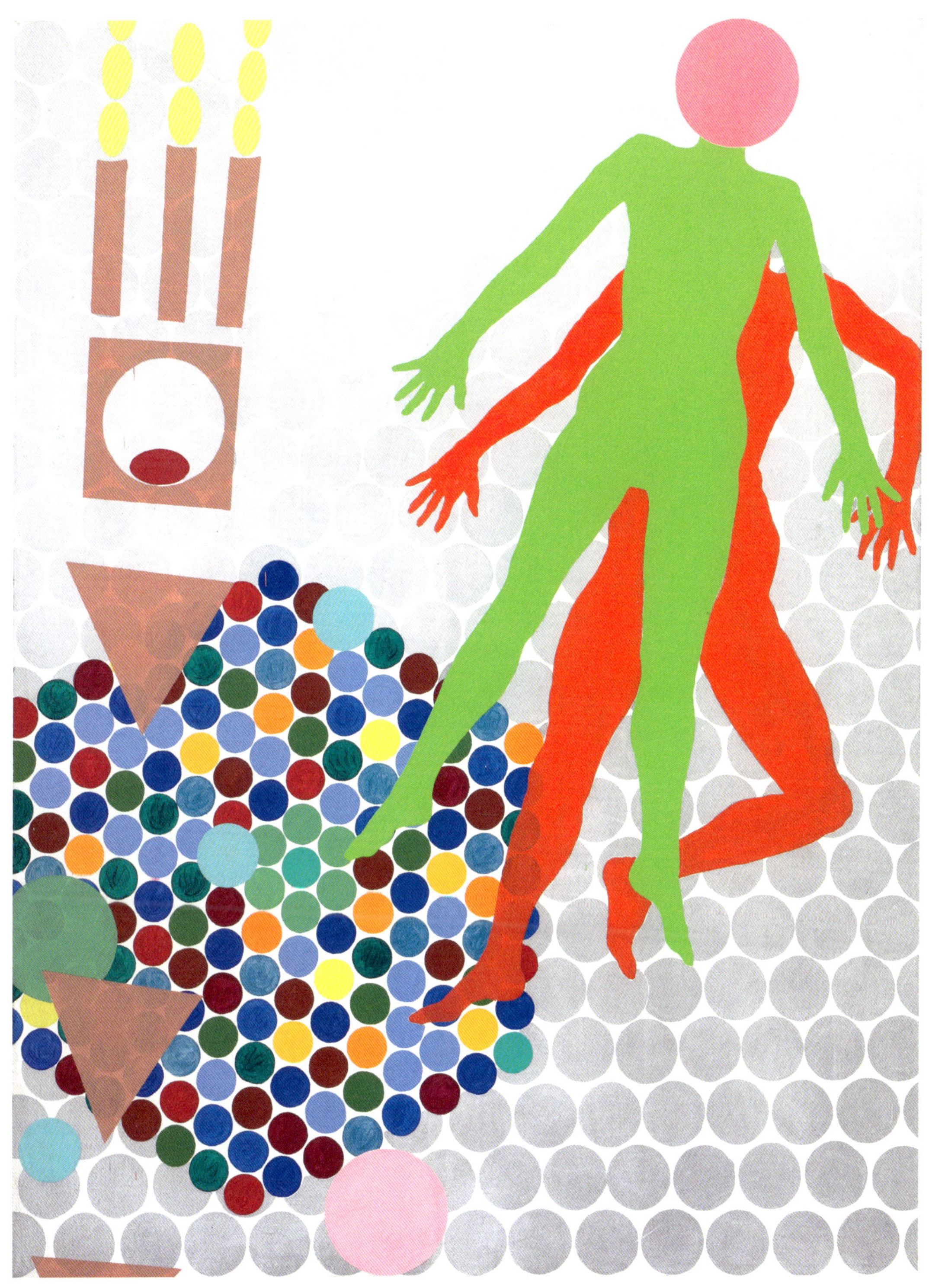

Fly Me to the Moon, 1963
Oil and acrylic on canvas
244 × 184.3 cm

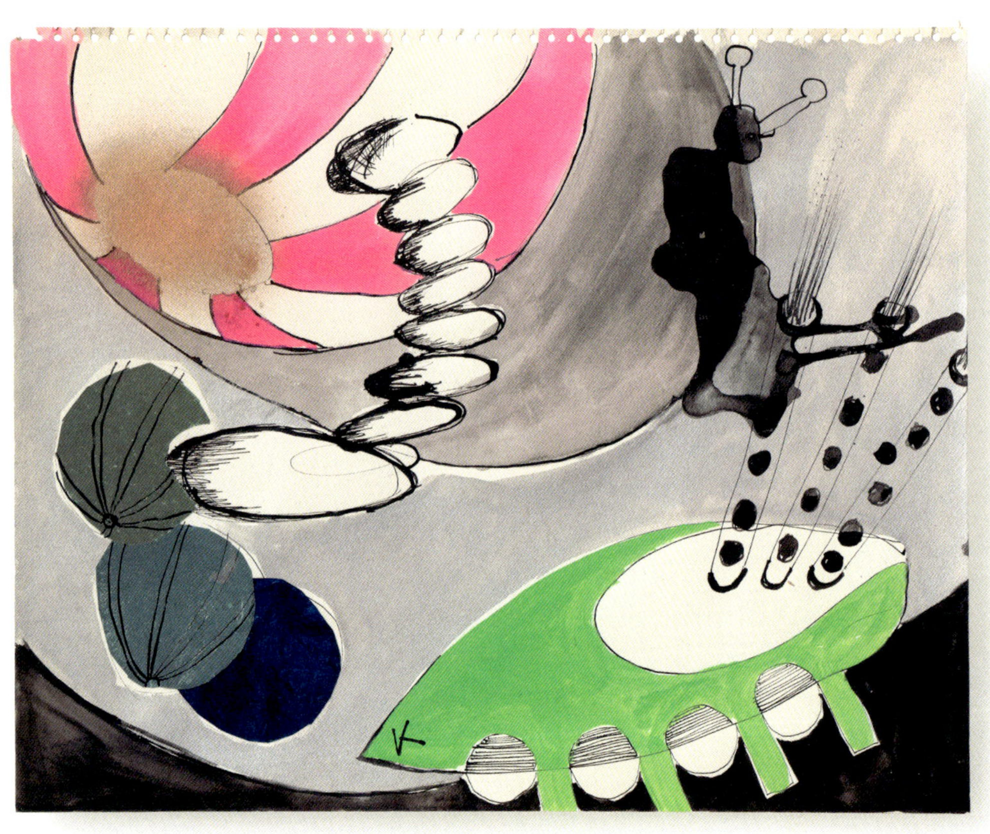

Untitled (Spaceship), c. 1963
Acrylic, enamel, India ink and foil on paper
33 × 41.5 cm

Hungriger Totenkopf, c. 1986
Glazed ceramics with mixed media and acrylic on wood
50 × 53 × 19.6 cm

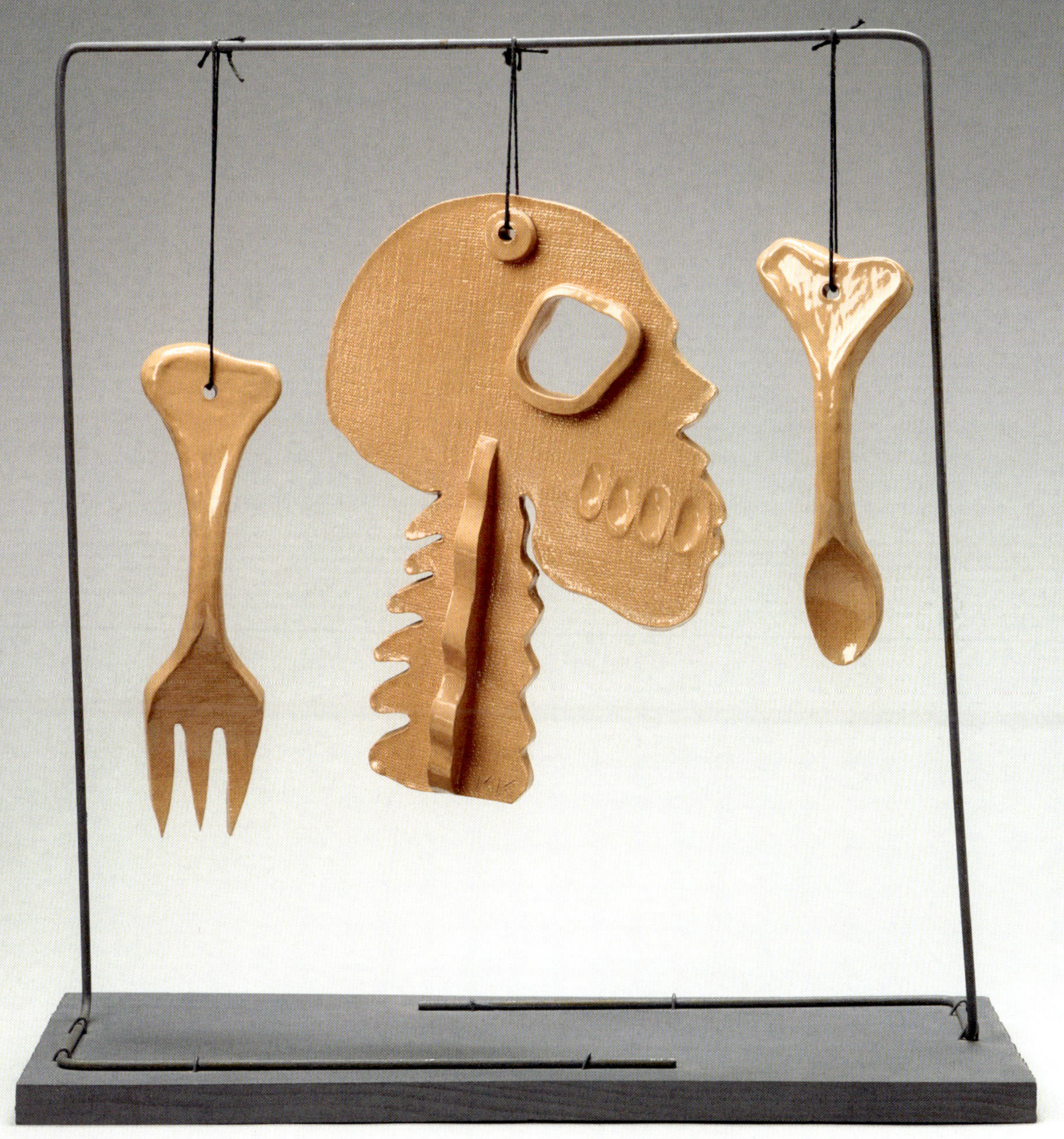

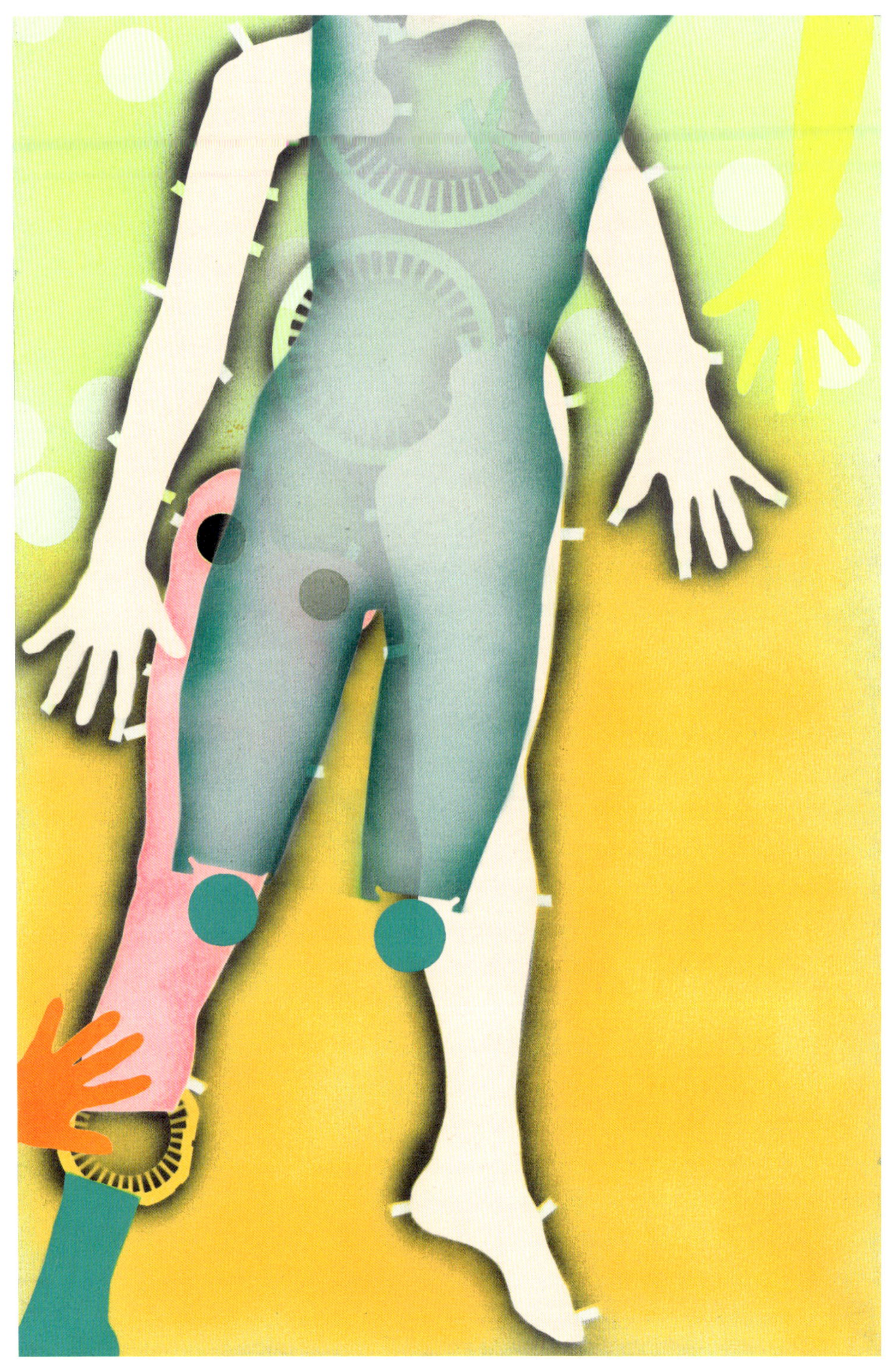

Liquid Injection Thrust, c. 1965
Oil and acrylic on canvas
139.3 × 93.4 cm

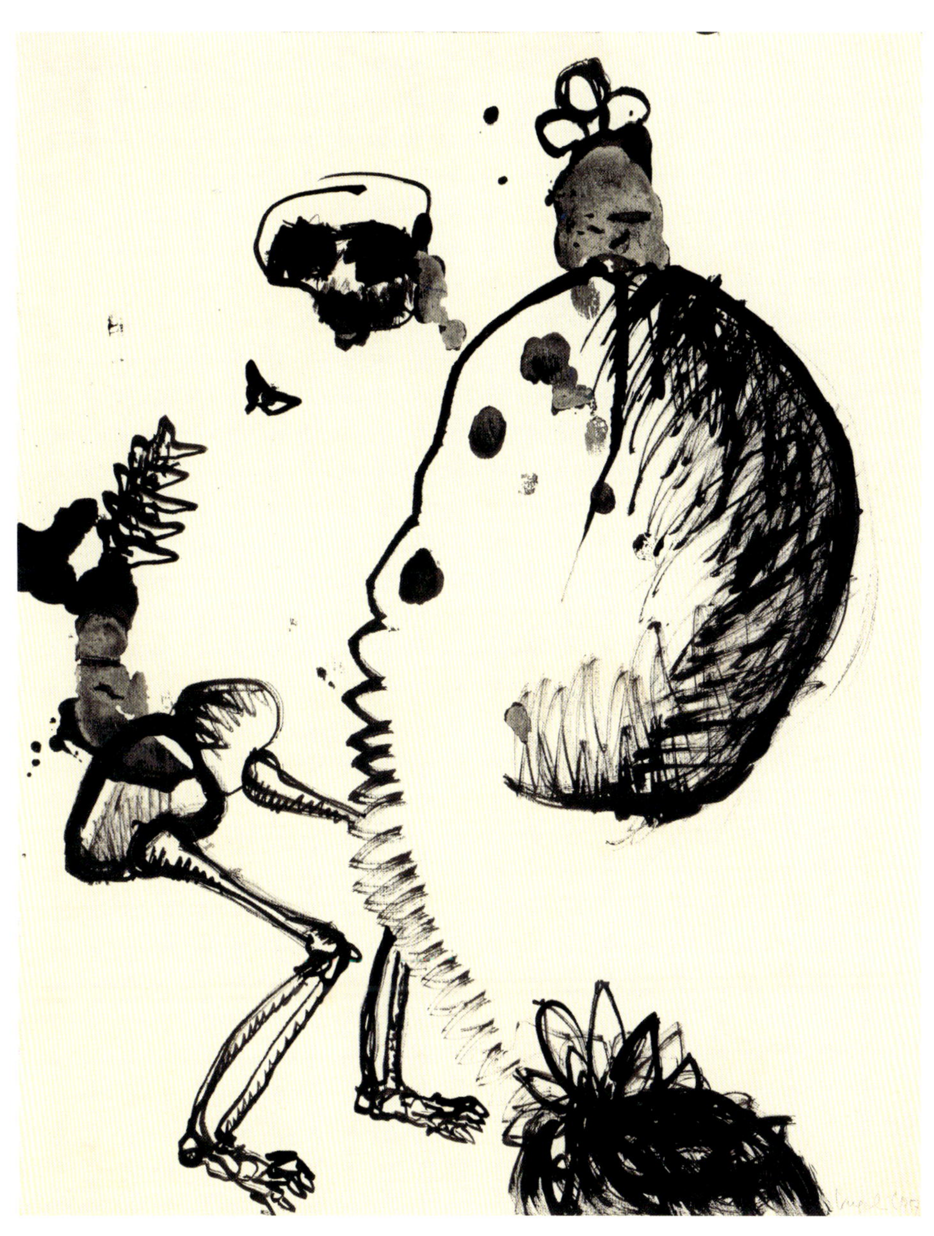

Untitled (Skeleton), 1957
India ink on paper
51.3 × 40.2 cm

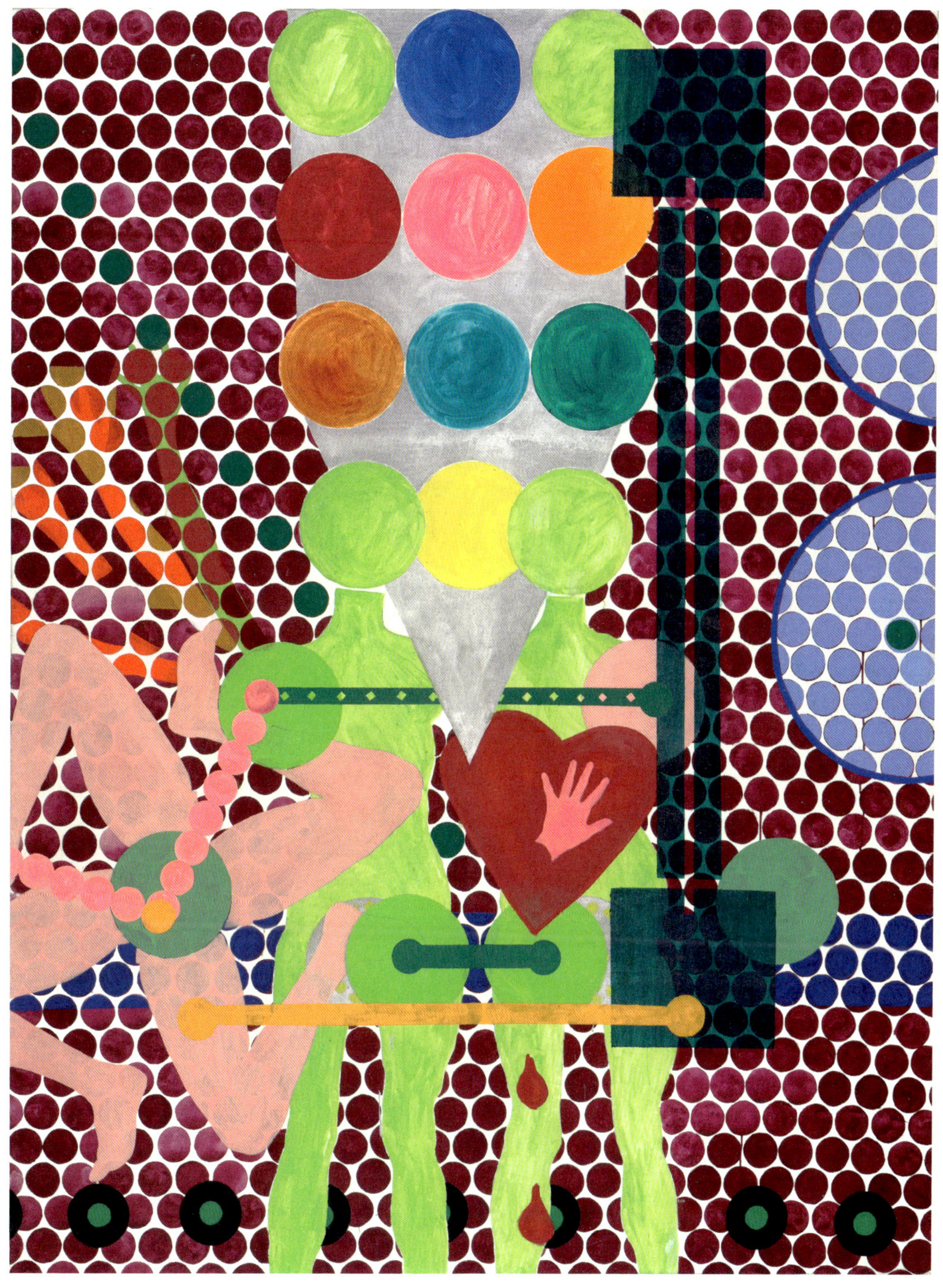

Machine, 1963
Oil and acrylic on canvas
244.5 × 184 cm

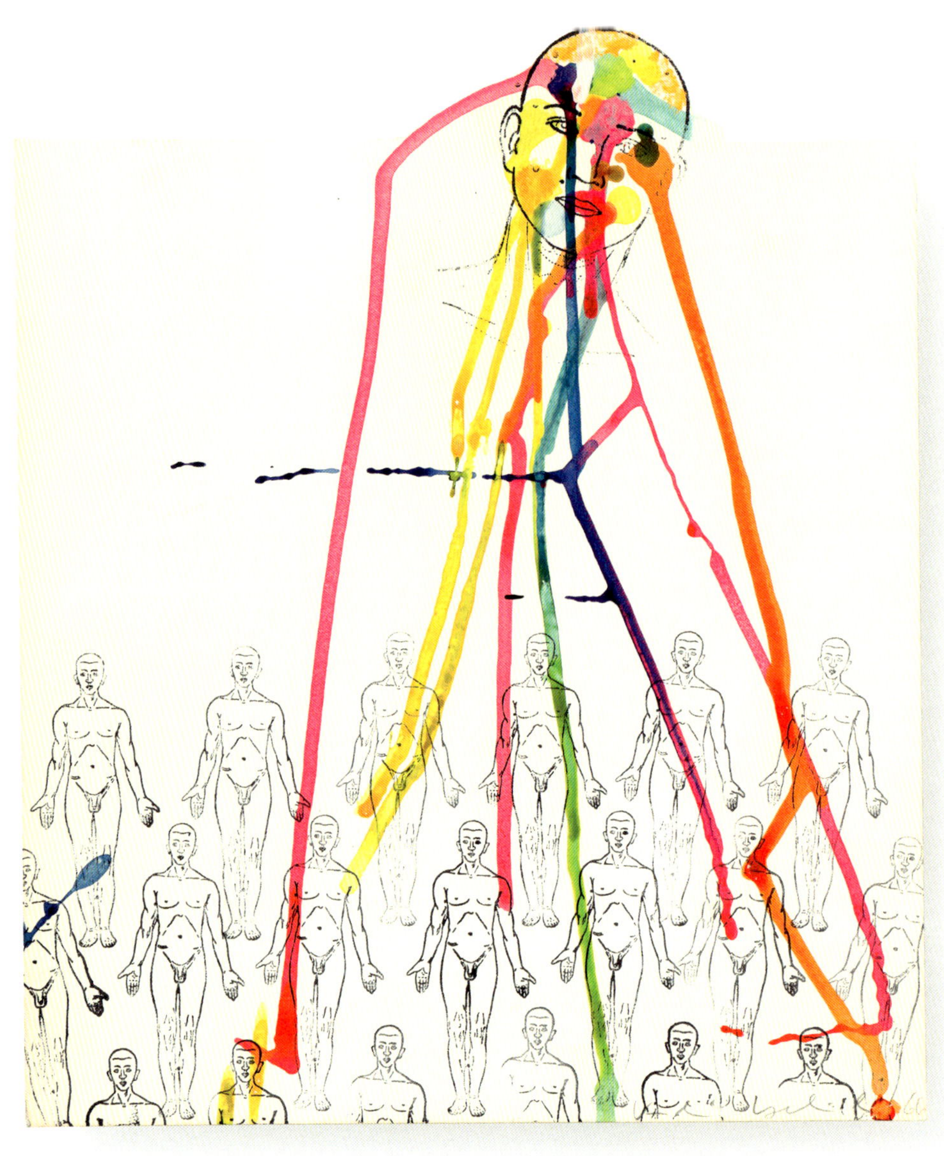

Robots, 1967
Ink on paper
32.5 × 27.5 cm

George, c. 1966
Fibreglass, chromed steel and mixed media
162.9 × 97.5 × 114 cm

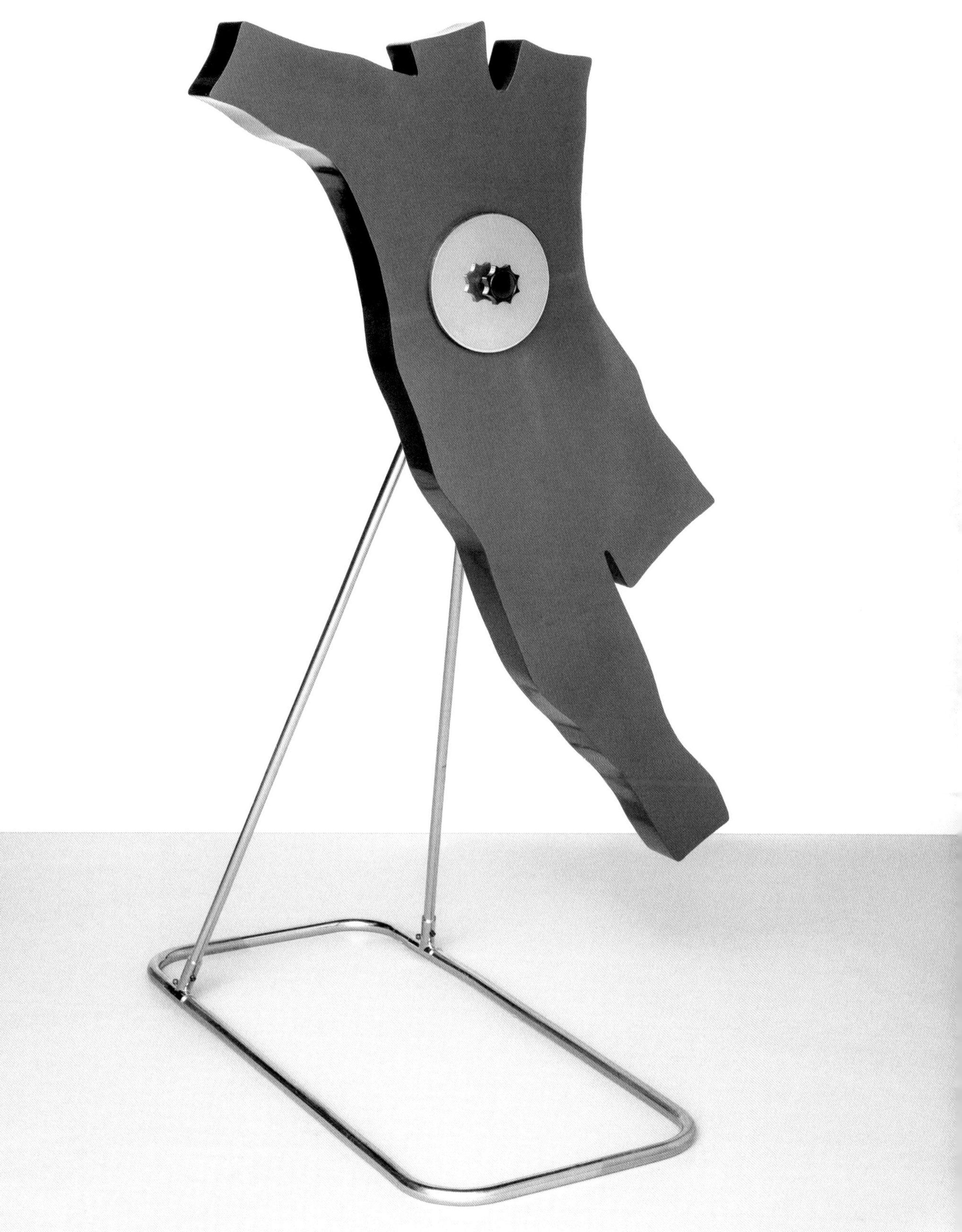

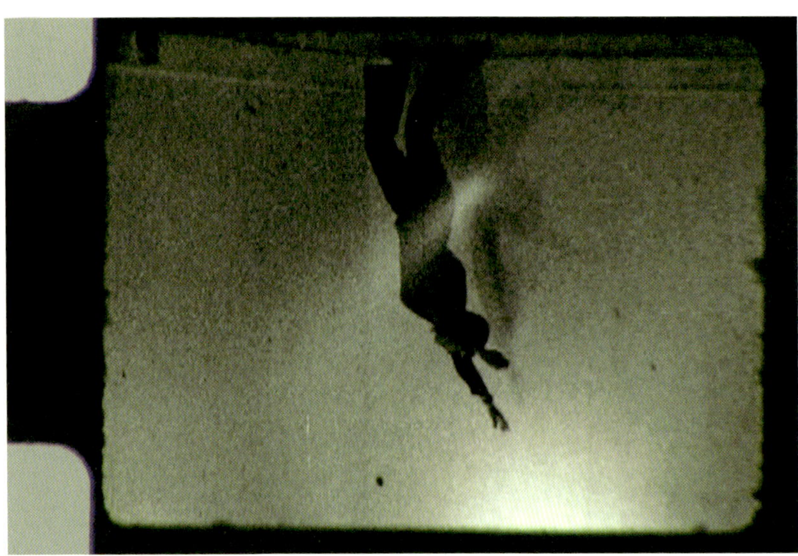

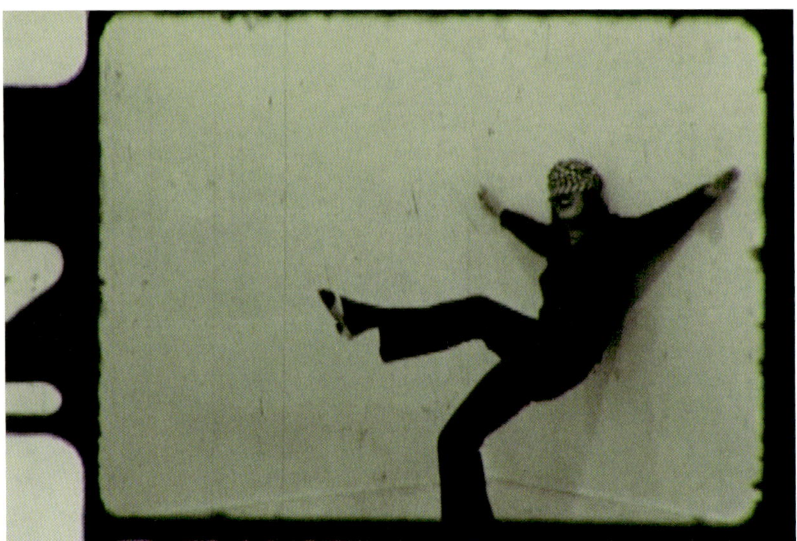

Untitled (Floating), c. 1964
8mm black and white film
0:37 min

Untitled (Small hanging), 1968
Sheet vinyl, Plexiglas and acrylic on steel and wood
41.5 × 31.1 × 24.5 cm

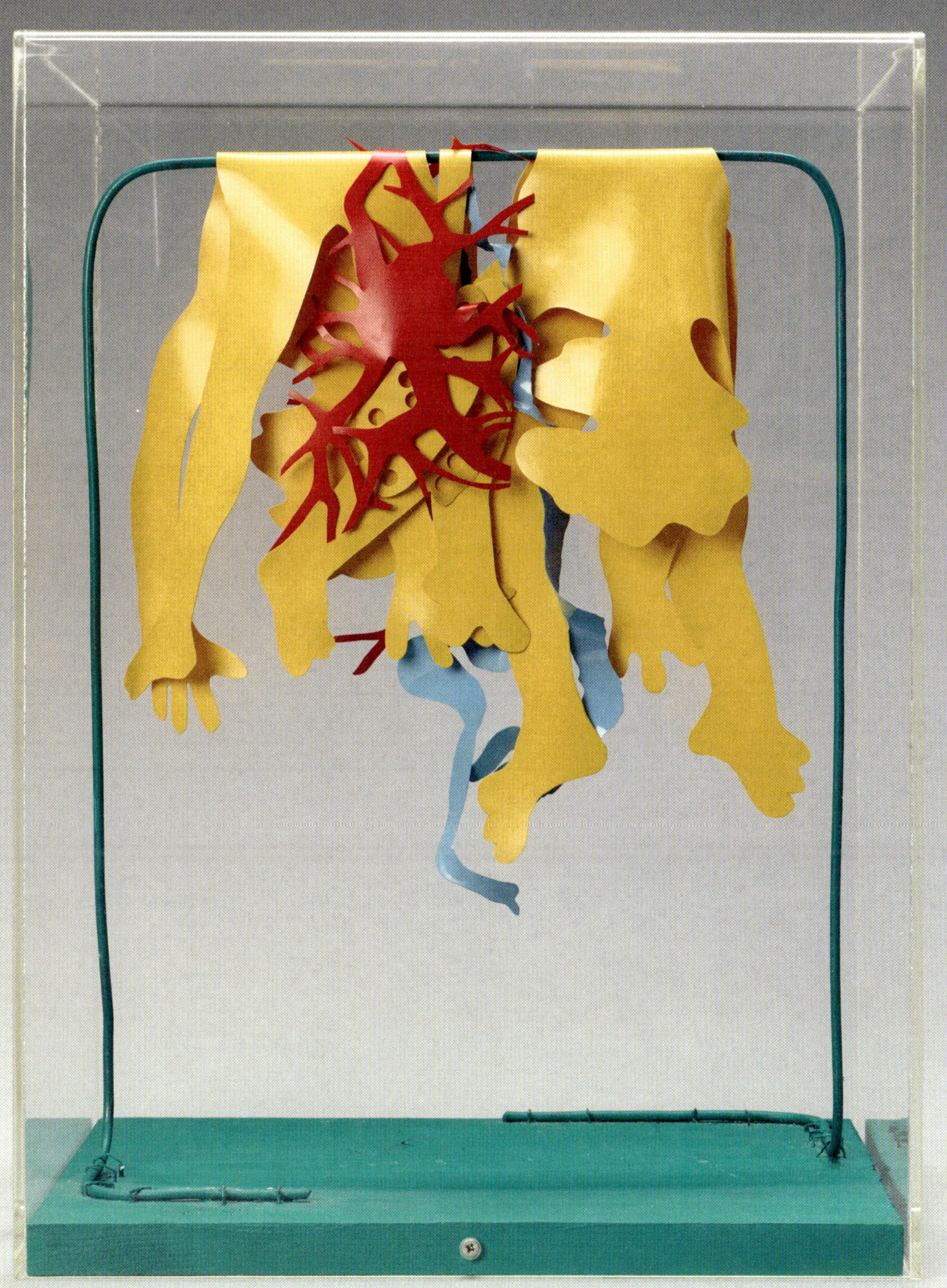

Bleiburg Skull, 1972
Sheet vinyl with mixed media
242 × 70 × 2.5 cm

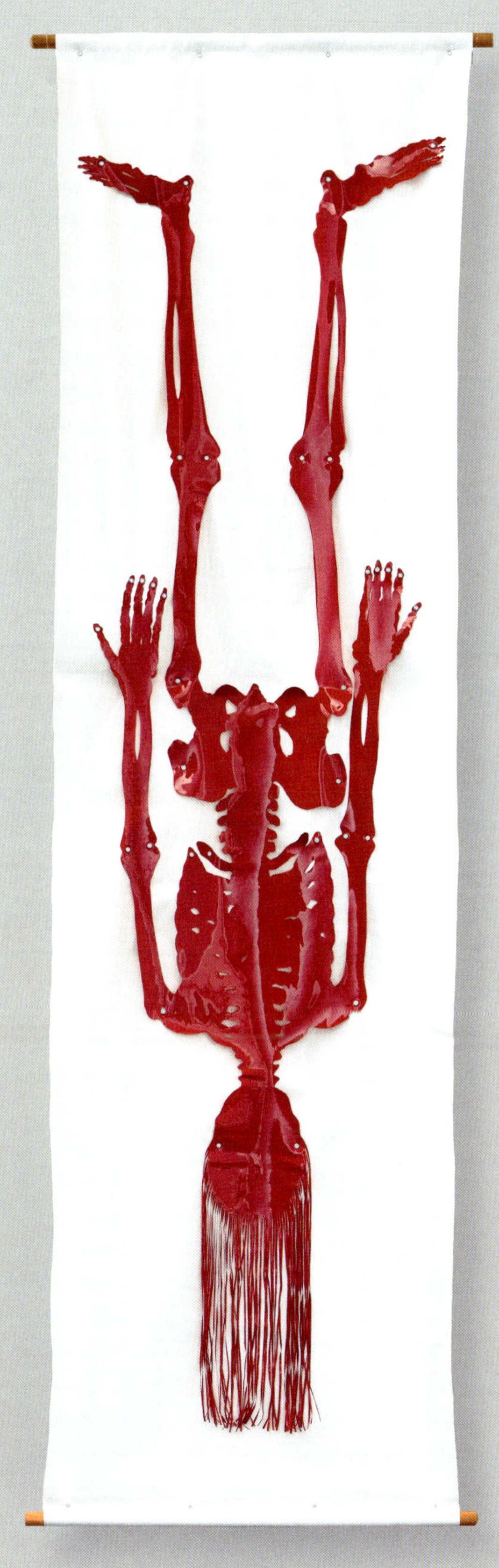

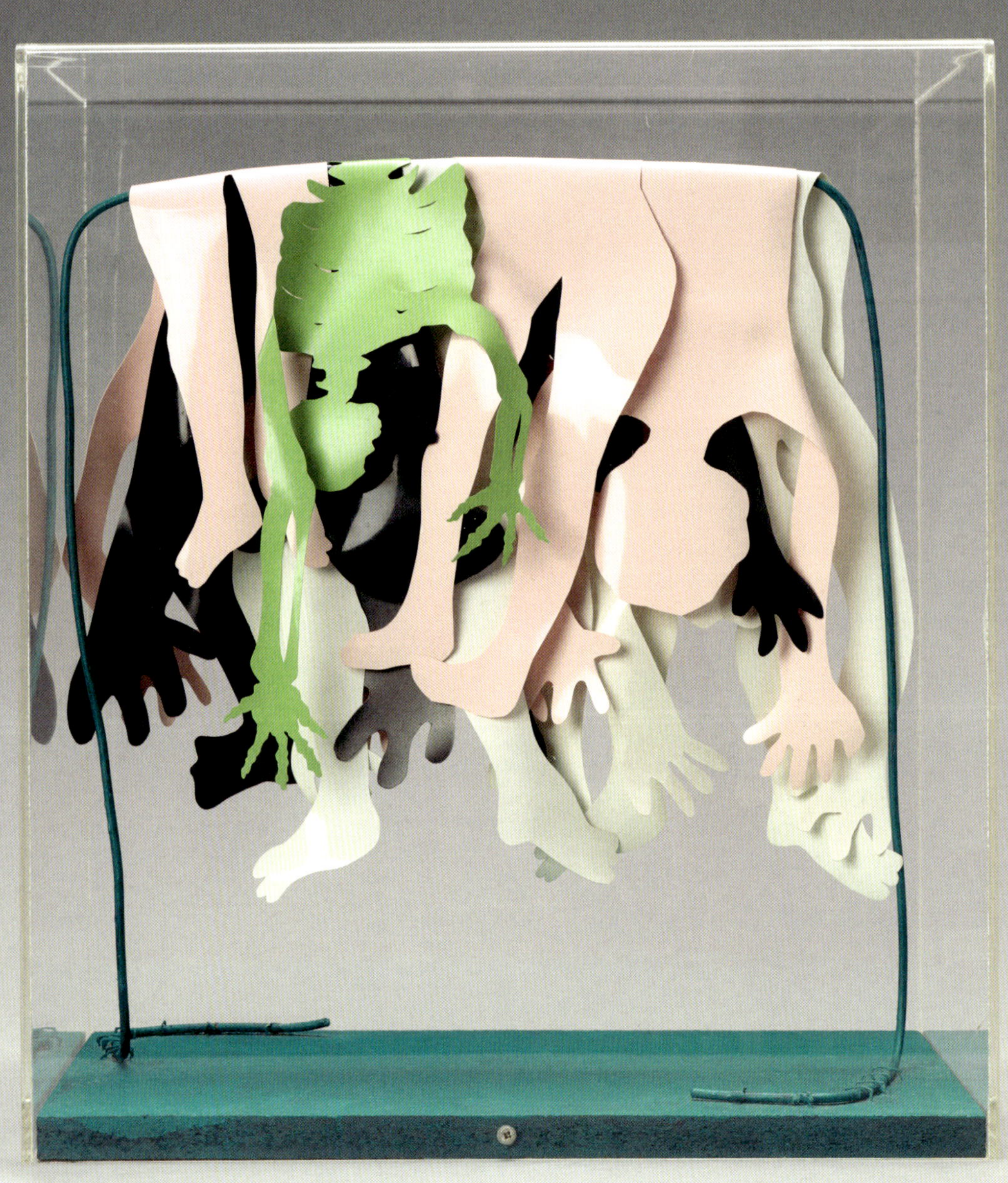

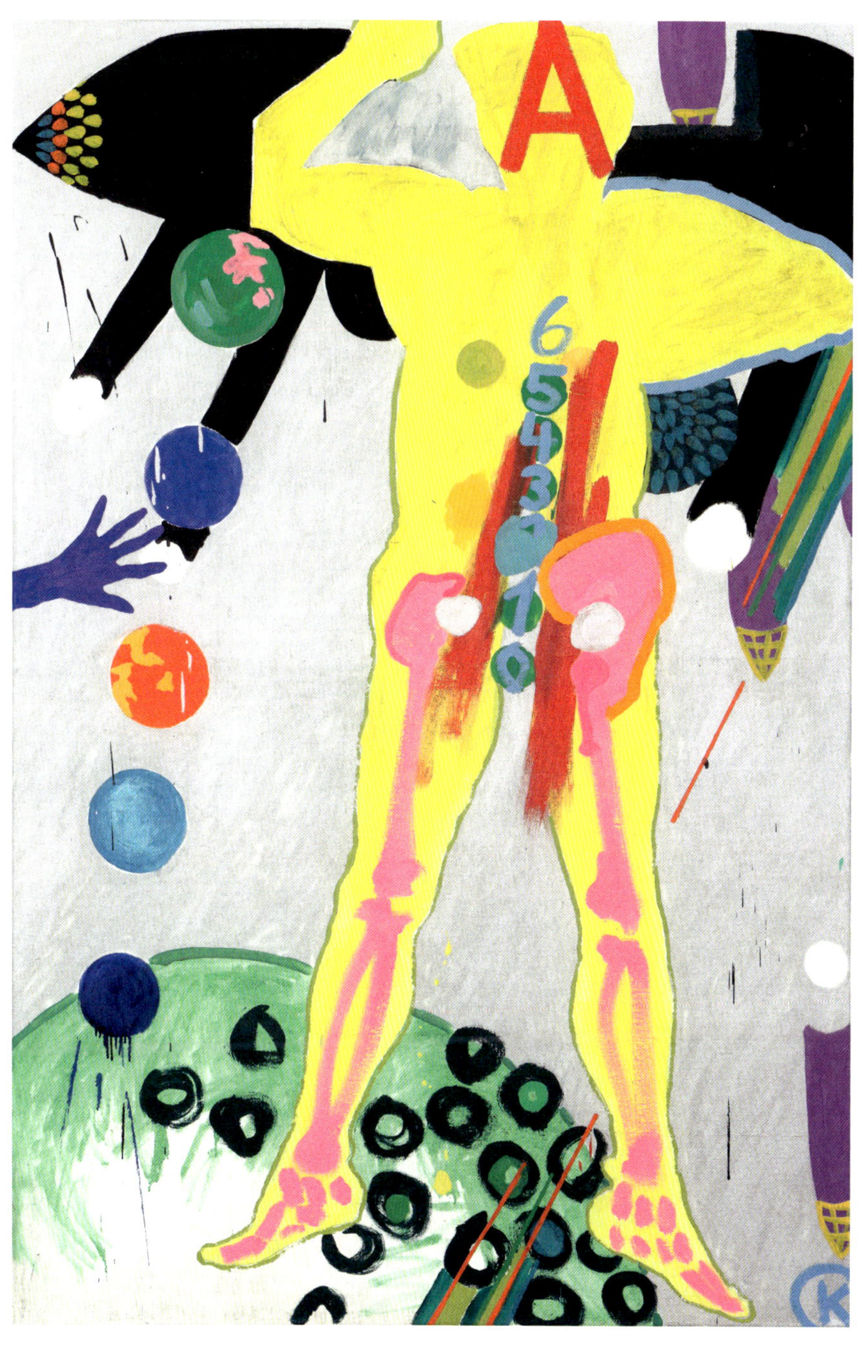

Untitled (Small hanging), 1968
Sheet vinyl, Plexiglas and acrylic on steel and wood
41.4 × 37.2 × 22.7 cm

Untitled (A), c. 1963
Oil and acrylic on canvas
180.6 × 120.5 cm

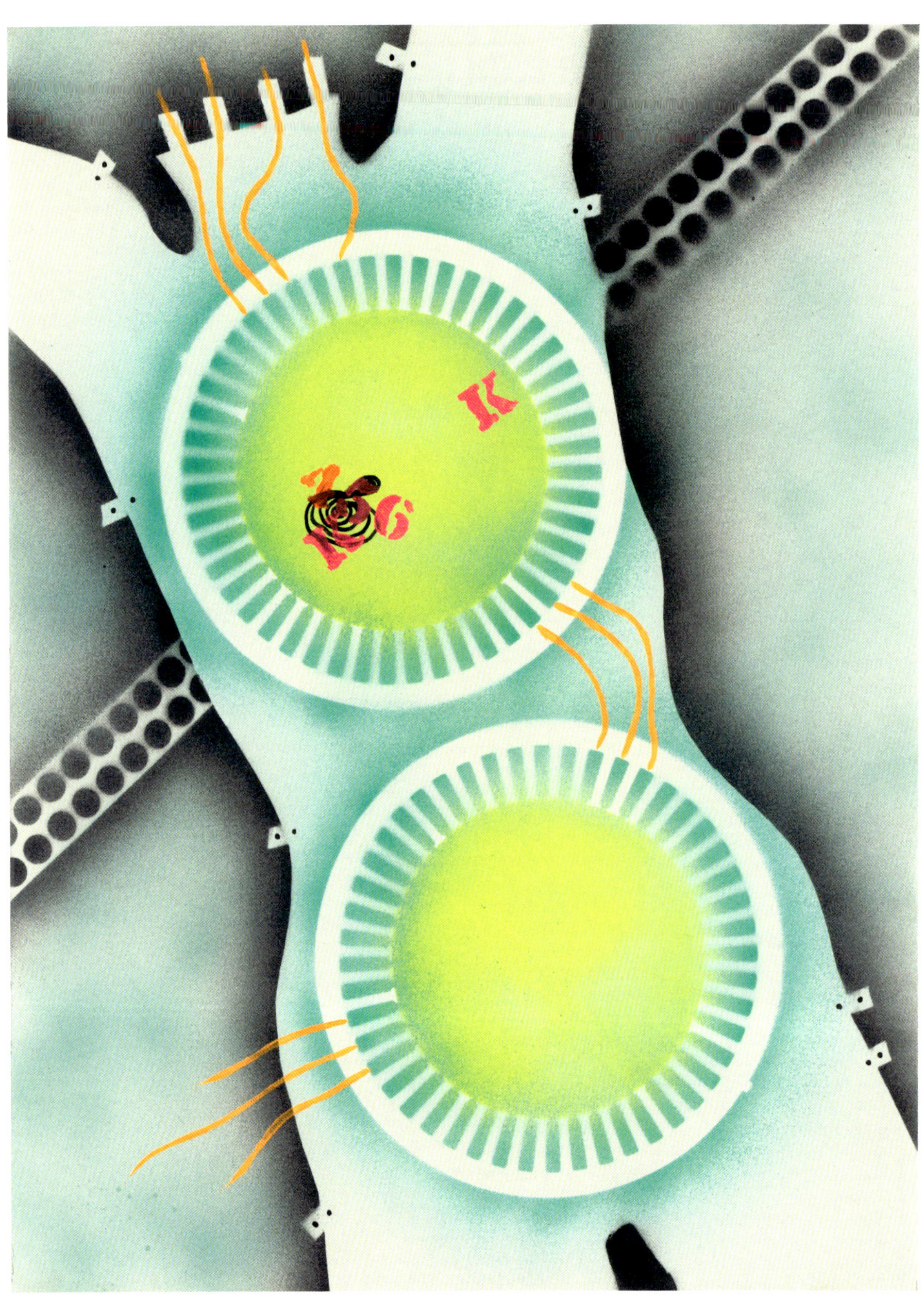

Transparent Woman, 1965
Acrylic, enamel, India ink and ink on paper
76 × 56.2 cm

Untitled (Hanging), c. 1970
Sheet vinyl with chromed steel hanger and mixed media
60.5 × 143.5 × 15.1 cm

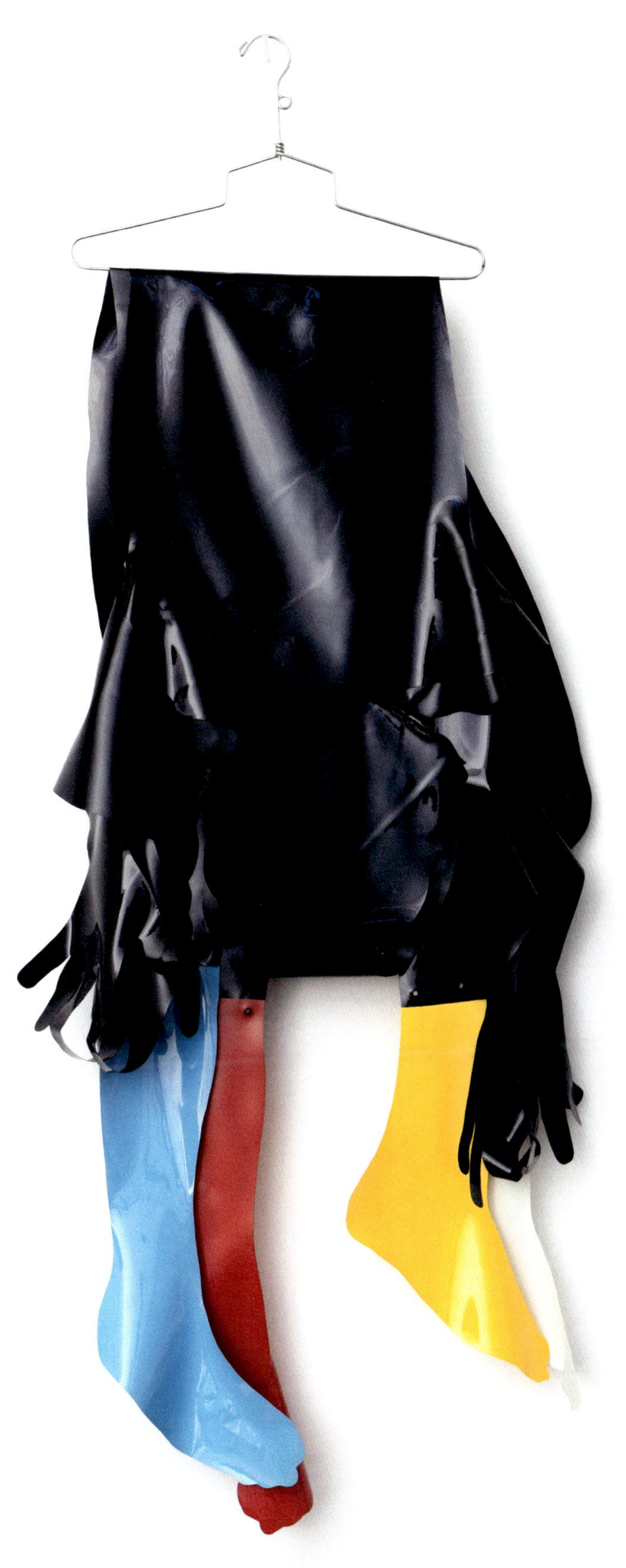

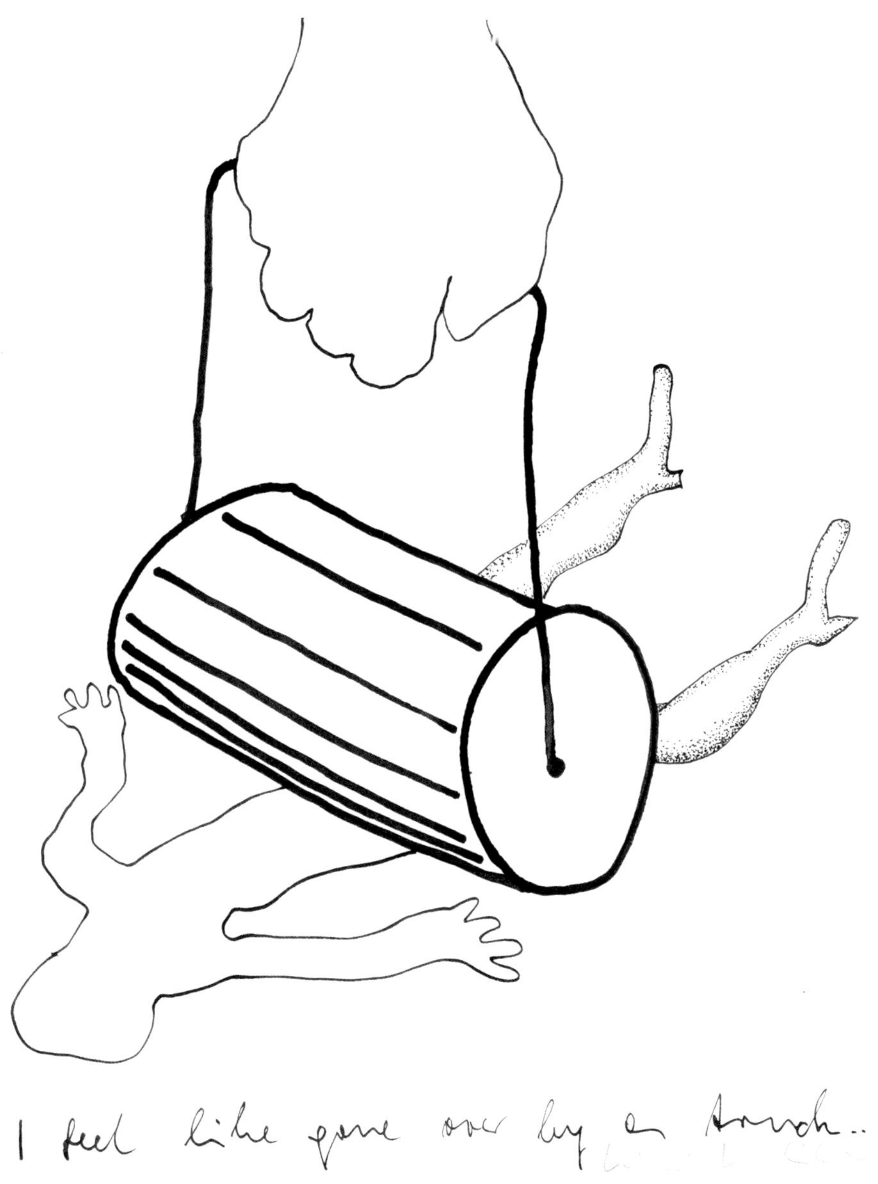

I Feel Like Gone Over by a Truck, 1970
India ink on paper
34.8 × 27.8 cm

Vibrations on a Composite Circuit, 1965
Oil and acrylic on canvas with mixed media
136.5 × 102 × 9 cm

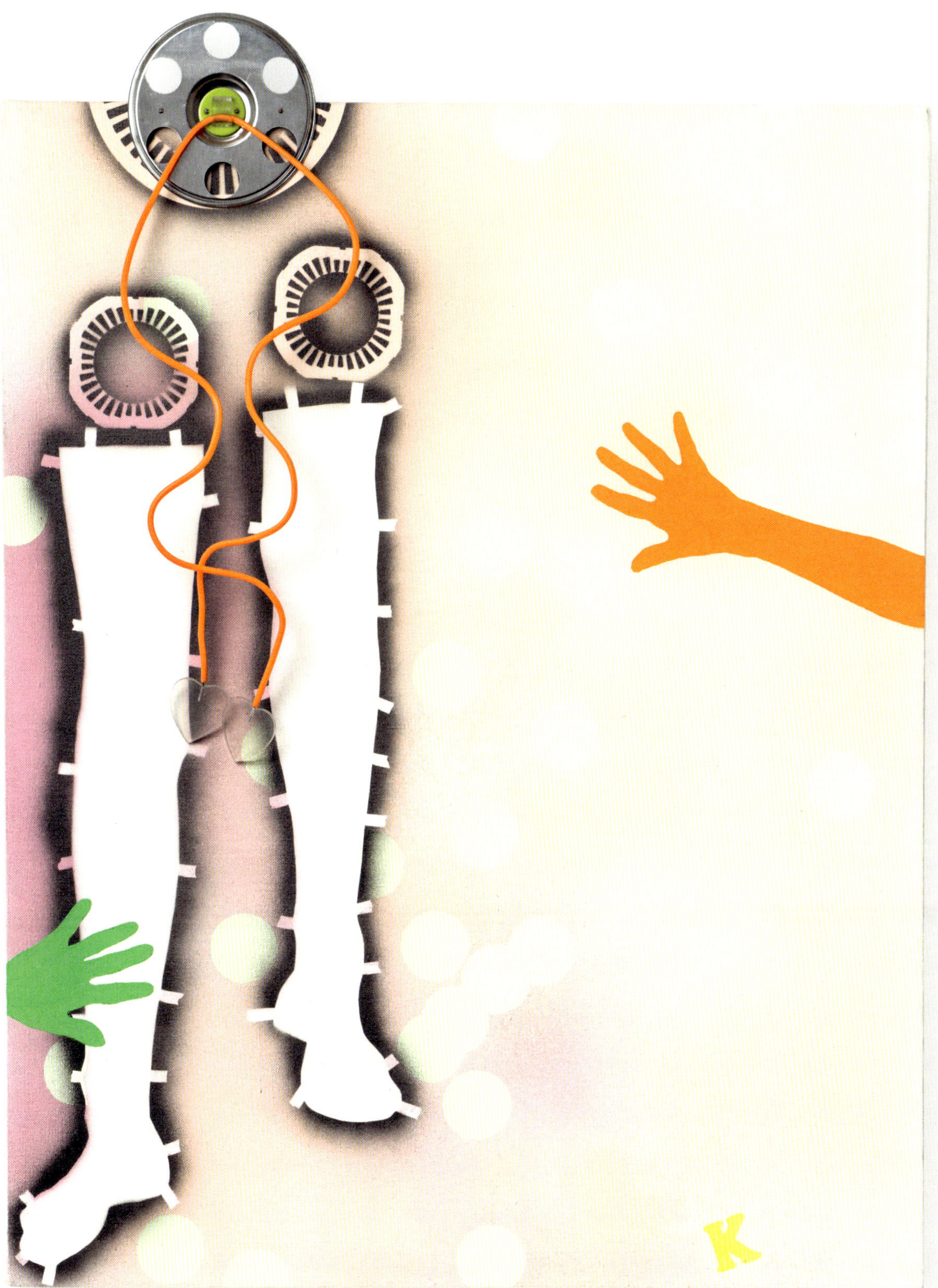

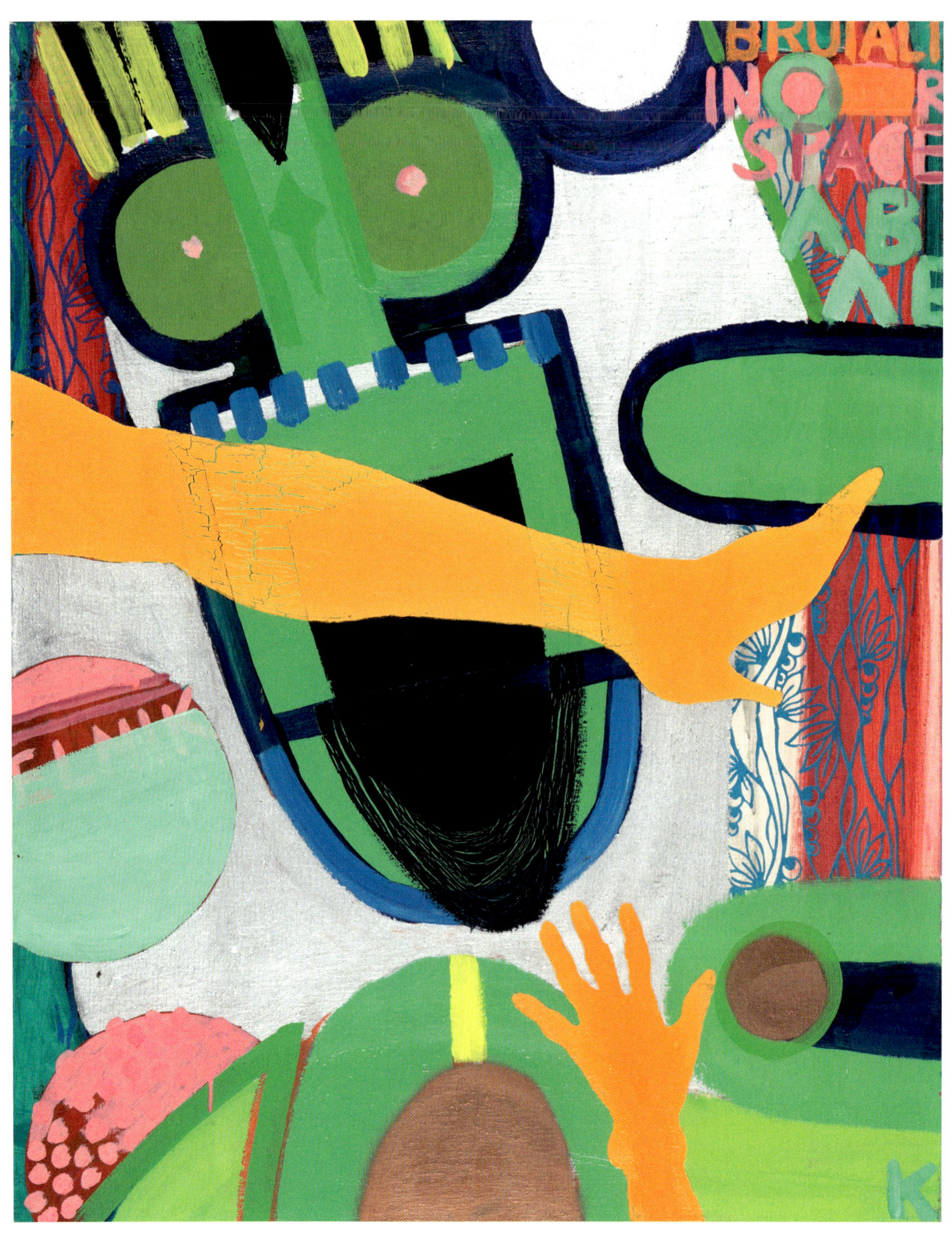

Brutal in Outer Space, c. 1962–63
Oil on canvas
92.2 × 73.7 cm

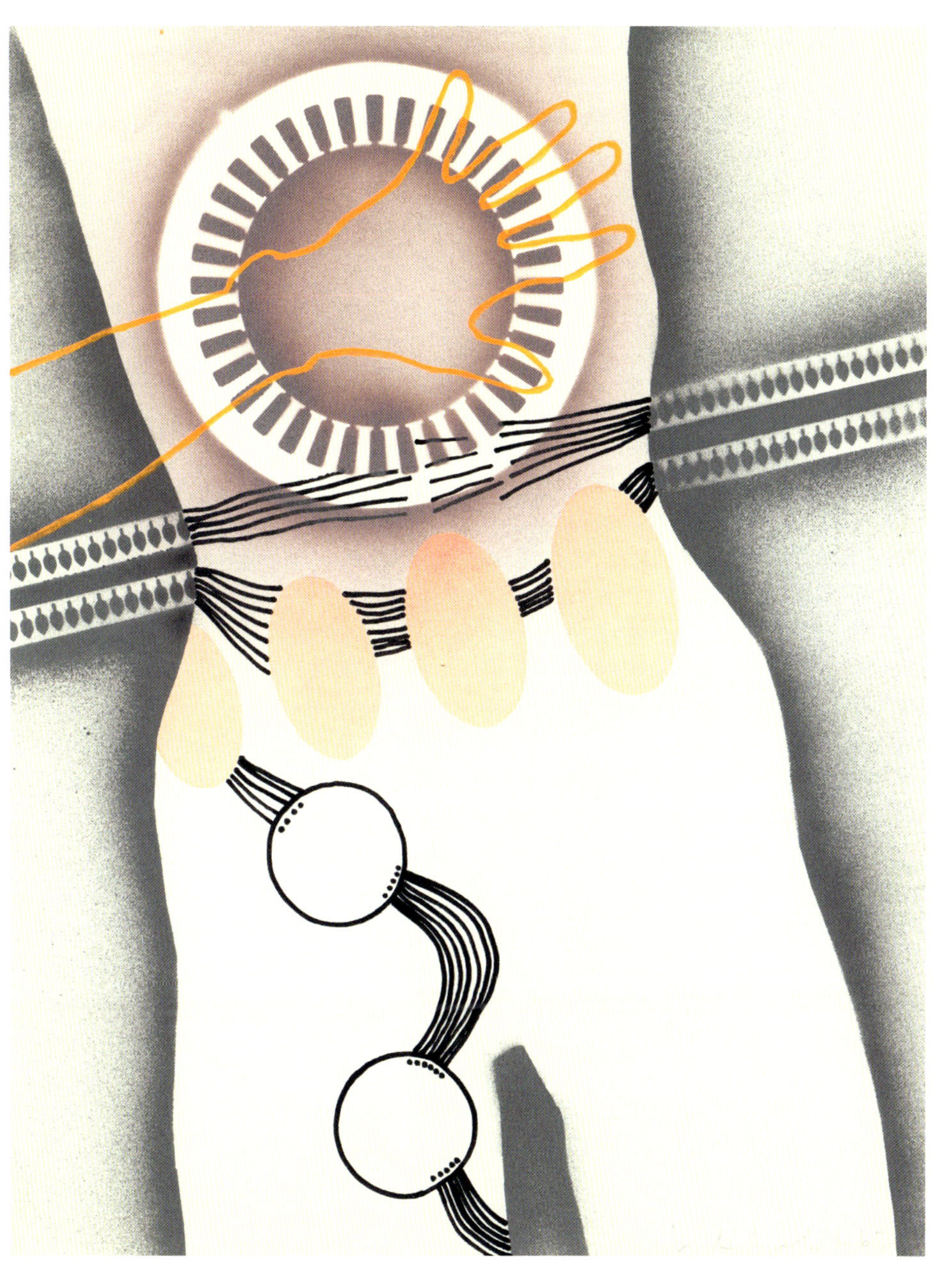

Untitled (Robot), 1965
Acrylic, enamel, India ink and ink on paper
65.2 × 50 cm

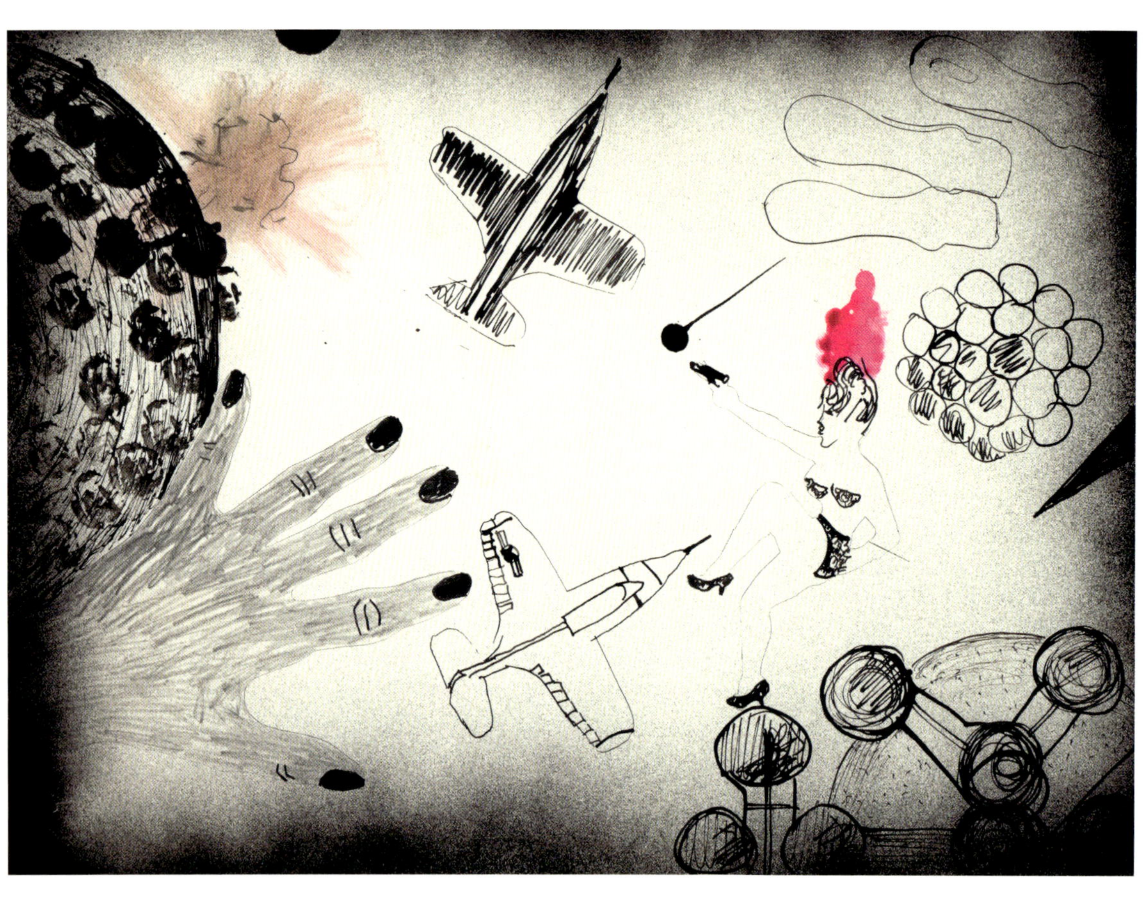

Untitled (Space), c. 1963
Acrylic, enamel and India ink on paper
33.1 × 45.1 cm

Fly Me to the Moon

The Western world is imploding. During the mechanical ages we had extended our bodies in space. Today, after more than a century of electric technology, we have extended our central nervous system itself in a global embrace, abolishing both space and time as far as our planet is concerned.[1]

Marshall McLuhan

Until recently Kiki Kogelnik was little known beyond her native Austria. Despite creating hundreds of remarkable, phantasmagorical paintings and sculptures during the heyday of Pop art in New York – alongside friends like Claes Oldenburg and Roy Lichtenstein – Kogelnik's work had been overlooked for decades.

Although widely characterised as a Pop artist, Kogelnik has rarely appeared in the countless exhibitions around the world examining the Pop art movement throughout the last 50 years. There are many reasons why this might be so. As a female artist operating in the patriarchal art world of 1960s New York, Kogelnik found it more difficult to gain recognition for her work than her male counterparts.[2] She did not have commercial representation, nor sell a great deal of work in her lifetime, which meant that collectors were not invested in promoting her work. It was also the case that American institutions at this time rarely supported European artists through exhibitions or acquisitions. As Kogelnik was omitted from major exhibitions, catalogues and retrospectives, the likelihood of future curators encountering her practice lessened over time.

Recently, however, this has begun to change thanks to a new wave of curators undertaking reassessments of the art-historical canon and Kogelnik's work is now being highlighted in exhibitions throughout Europe. These include *POWER UP – Female Pop Art* at Kunsthalle Wien, Vienna in 2010, curated by

---

[1] Marshall McLuhan, 'Challenge and Collapse: The Nemesis of Creativity' from 'Understanding Media', published in Charles Harrison and Paul Wood (eds.), *Art in Theory 1900–1990: An Anthology of Changing Ideas*, Blackwell, Oxford, 1996, p. 740.

[2] Art critic and historian Hal Foster has noted that female Pop artists failed to garner critical acclaim because women were objectified by Pop art itself; 'women could not act as its principal subjects in large part because they were conscripted as its primary objects, even its primary fetishes'. Hal Foster, *The First Pop Age: Painting and Subjectivity in the Art of Hamilton, Lichtenstein, Warhol, Richter and Ruscha*, Princeton University Press, Princeton, NJ and Oxford, 2012, p. 15.

Angela Stief, which featured work by Dorothy Iannone, Evelyne Axell, Niki de Saint Phalle, Marisol, Sister Corita and Jann Haworth as well as Kogelnik. *The World Goes Pop*, upcoming at Tate Modern, London, later this year, presents a 'global story of pop art' and will include Kogelnik's work. Such exhibitions do a valuable job in bringing lesser-known work to a wider audience. However, by presenting female and non-Western art practices separately from canonical exhibitions and collections, they also risk marginalising these artists to peripheral positions. It might do these artists a greater service by including their works in and amongst the work of their more famous counterparts.

However, that undertaking is beyond the purview of this project, which aims to present the work of a single artist in depth. *Fly Me to the Moon*, the exhibition at Modern Art Oxford, is the first solo presentation of Kogelnik's practice in the Anglophone world and takes as its focus the relationship between the body and technology, looking in particular at her practice from the 1960s and early 1970s.[3] The exhibition takes place in the context of a year-long programme at the gallery examining the impact of rapid technological change on individual agency in the twenty-first century. Produced in a time of great social and political upheaval, Kogelnik's work provides a valuable historical perspective on the dawn of a new society increasingly dominated by machines and artificial production.

Born in Bleiburg, Austria in 1935, Kogelnik studied fine art in Vienna between 1954–58 where she made abstract paintings alongside peers like Arnulf Rainer, Maria Lassnig and Josef Mikl. Kogelnik quickly established herself as a maverick figure on the arts scene, and many of her fellow artists considered her work to be indecorously bright and colourful.[4] Growing restless, Kogelnik turned to America for inspiration and her work began to show the influence of the looser, more gestural work of artists such as Willem de Kooning and Sam Francis, who she later befriended. Francis encouraged Kogelnik to move to America, which she did in 1961.

On leaving the depressed economic climate of postwar Europe, Kogelnik encountered the bustling, capitalist wonderland of New York, which hosted a

[3] This thematic lens precludes the inclusion of Kogelnik's more overtly feminist practice from the 1970s during which time she produced a number of paintings of female figures, critiquing the representation of women in mainstream media.

[4] Helga Ripper, 'Kiki Kogelnik. Schere statt Pinsel', in *ARTgenossen*, Austrian Broadcasting Corporation (ORF), 16 October 1994.

vibrant and progressive artistic scene. Around this time, artists were beginning to draw on the subjects and symbols of everyday life, excited by the possibilities of new media, television, radio, commercials, billboards and the mass dissemination of this information. There was a prevailing sense that Pop art was an American phenomenon, despite the increasing interest of British artists in commercial imagery that was happening around the same time.[5]

Kogelnik's work soon reflected her changed environment. Like her peers, she was inspired by Dada and Duchamp and began incorporating readymades into her practice to reflect the radically different cultural landscape of America, adhering household objects to the surfaces of her work in a manner reminiscent of Robert Rauschenberg's 'Combines' or Jim Dine's early multimedia paintings. Eschewing abstraction for figuration, and muted shades for vivid colour, once in America Kogelnik developed a visual language and iconography that was distinctly her own, with works like *Machine* (1963) employing dots, stencils, abstract shapes and lurid colours in dramatic and startling juxtapositions. Particular motifs, such as the toothed, cog-like, circle and the stamped initial 'K', recur across works like *Vibrations on a Composite Circuit* (1965) and *Transparent Woman* (1965). While this repetition might appear to suggest the mechanised production of the factory line á la Andy Warhol, Kogelnik relied in fact on a great deal of handicraft, using hammers, saws, torches, belt sanders, riveters and scissors to execute her works.[6]

Kogelnik's formal innovations were undoubtedly unique, but it is her persistent representation of the delights and terrors of space travel that are of special interest here. In paintings like *Brutal in Outer Space* (c. 1962–63) and *Fly Me to the Moon* (1963) effervescent, celestial bodies hurtle through the sky, encountering a jumble of mysterious flying forms. Primary coloured circles and elemental triangles suggest spaceships and planets in orbit. These shapes are further delineated in a series of works on paper which more clearly depict jet-propelled rockets and intergalactic voyagers. Drawings like *Untitled (Space)* (c. 1963) present outsize hands reaching across vibrant humming landscapes. Pirate spaceships bear down upon strange galaxies in *Space* (1963), while in *Untitled (Nescafe Nescafe)* (c. 1963) rockets adorned with advertising venture into the stratosphere.

---

[5] Bettina Funcke notes the rise of the 'catchphrase' of the 'Americanisation' of culture in the postwar period when TVs entered private homes in huge numbers. Bettina Funcke, *Pop or Populus: Art Between High and Low*, Sternberg Press, Berlin, 2009.

[6] Alexandra Hennig, 'Kiki Kogelnik. Robot Fantasies, or How the Bombs Learned to Love,' Kunsthalle Krems, Krems, 2013, p. 38 from Jo Anna Isaak, 'Hangings 1967–70. New York Hangings', in Kiki Kogelnik and Peter Noever (eds.), *Kiki Kogelnik: Hangings*, exhibition catalogue, MAK, Vienna, 1996, p. 22.

Kogelnik was not alone in her fascination with the new technologies of the 1960s. During this era of the space race and Cold War nuclear paranoia, there was a proliferation of popular novels, films and artworks drawing on the images and narratives of sci-fi, from Stanley Kubrick's *2001: A Space Odyssey* (1968) to Warhol's *Silver Clouds* (1966). Science fiction offered artists of all disciplines a language with which to articulate the rapid new advances of their time. As the critic and theorist of Pop art Lawrence Alloway wrote, 'SF aids the assimilation of the mounting technical facts of this century'.[7] For Susan Sontag, the incorporation by artists of new industrial materials and methods challenged the traditional boundaries between art and science, transforming art itself into 'an instrument for modifying consciousness and organising new modes of sensibility'.[8] This became all the more urgent in a decade in which the human body exceeded its capabilities through machines, using rockets, synthetic space suits and computerised equipment to leave the planet, explore outer space and, potentially, encounter alien life forms.

In the mid 1960s Kogelnik's work took an increasingly critical tone, moving from the loosely modelled and primary-coloured figures of her early work to harder-edged forms and acid hues. In *Ikarus* (1965) Kogelnik's critique of this 'brave new world' is inherent in her adoption of a doomed mythological figure as emblematic of space travel. Kogelnik suggests that man's curiosity and desire to transcend earthly boundaries could have devastating effects; there is an impending sense of doom in Ikarus's tumbling form, fated for an early demise. The body in *Liquid Injection Thrust* (c. 1965) appears similarly volatile; whilst it is successfully being propelled upward (or, at least, upright), it has, rather disturbingly, become separated into four stencilled limbs with mechanical-looking innards taking the place of human organs.

Kogelnik's use of kaleidoscopic pattern to represent the astronaut's paradoxical balance of deathly stillness and immense speed recalls Roland Barthes's description of the new kind of motion performed by the 'jet-man', which is traumatic for our earth-bound senses to behold: 'The jet-man… is defined by a coenaesthesis of motionlessness… Motion is no longer the optical perception of points and surfaces; it has become a kind of vertical disorder, made of contractions, black-outs, terrors and faints; it is no longer a gliding but an inner devastation,

[7] Lawrence Alloway, 'The Arts and the Mass Media', published in Charles Harrison and Paul Wood, *op.cit.*, 1996, p.702.

[8] Susan Sontag, 'One culture and the new sensibility', *Against Interpretation*, Vintage, London, 2001, pp.296–97.

[9] Roland Barthes, *Mythologies*, Vintage, London, 2000, p.71

an unnatural perturbation, a motionless crisis of bodily consciousness'.[9] Ever experimental, Kogelnik also used film to evoke the disorienting effects of flight. In *Untitled (Floating)* (c. 1964), she performed a series of movements in the studio before an 8 mm camera turned upside down to mimic the weightlessness of space travel.

Marshall McLuhan described the new media of the twentieth century as an amplification and extension of the self, constituting 'huge collective surgery carried out on social body with complete disregard for antiseptics'.[10] Like McLuhan, Kogelnik adopted surgical metaphors in her work to characterise the explosive effect of this future world. Arms are severed from the torso in the painting *Artificial Hand* (1966) and mechanical prostheses prop up the organs in *Untitled (Pump for heart)* (1965). Drawings like *Robots* (1966) dehumanise the figure even further, illustrating the dispassionate decapitation of a line-up of identical human bodies with visible organs and skeletal systems.

Towards the end of the 1960s, Kogelnik's slicing of the human form manifested itself in a series of sculptures known as 'Hangings', which she created by drawing the outline of friends and family onto sheets of paper to create a stencil. This was then used to cut out a shape in bright-coloured vinyl which was hung on a hanger or from a peg. For instance, the small cut-outs of *Mono* (c. 1970) were generated from the figure of her young son and *Claes* (c. 1970) from the artist's friend and famous Pop artist Claes Oldenburg. This choice of display was inspired by the clothes rails that Kogelnik regularly saw wheeled through the Garment District in New York near to where her studio was located.

Some hangings such as *Untitled (Small hanging)* (1968) were overlaid with intricate networks resembling the body's nervous systems. The cheery colours of these works belie the disturbing effect of sagging bodies hung on racks, appearing as disposable as the fashion which usually adorned them. Kogelnik also explored the possibilities of the hanging form in a number of works on paper like *Ingredients Bags* (1970) which similarly represent the body as only the sum of its parts, a mere ingredient bag of organs, in a distressing and detached form.

[10] Marshall McLuhan, Introduction to 'Understanding Media', published in Charles Harrison and Paul Wood, *op.cit.*, p. 738.

By rendering the body in new plastics and displaying them as lifeless entities, Kogelnik pointed to the dehumanising effects of industrial mass-production in which humanity becomes subordinate to machines and to the inexorable march of scientific progress. The repetition of the forms in multiple hangings suggests that efficiency and profit might one day override human needs. Kogelnik continued to push the boundaries of her practice through experimenting with new materials, producing fibreglass sculptures such as *George* (c. 1966), ceramic sculptures and creating silkscreen prints on Plexiglas in works like *Untitled (Flight)* (1968), printed with fluorescent paint which becomes luminous when light is shone upon it.

The integration of body and synthetic forms in Kogelnik's work anticipated many of the possibilities awaiting humanity in the twentieth and twenty-first centuries, from prostheses and robots to cyborgs and artificial intelligence. These works create a dramatic, sensory experience which aids the viewer's reflection on the ethical implications of new technologies for humanity. Remarkably prescient for its time, Kogelnik embodies McLuhan's vision of the artist who 'picks up the message of cultural and technological challenge decades before its transforming impact occurs'.[11]

Indeed, Kogelnik's mounting concern regarding interplanetary and robotic technology is prophetic for today's digitally networked world, entirely reliant upon wireless, electronic communication at the expense of the natural environment. In her performance *Moonhappening* (1969), Kogelnik staged a live screen-printing to accompany Neil Armstrong's first steps on the moon, which was playing on a monitor in the gallery. It has been suggested that by closing the gap between the production of an artwork and its display and reception, Kogelnik prefigured the accelerated pace of media-saturated culture.[12] Works such as *Plug-in Hand* (c. 1967) anticipate the ever-present plugged-in and switched-on state of twenty-first-century society, constantly in the grip of mobile internet and social media. Kogelnik's exploration of the conflation of identity and 'the exteriorities of consumer life'[13] at the expense of our inner lives and imaginations seems more pertinent today than ever.

---

[11] Marshall McLuhan, 'Challenge and Collapse: The Nemesis of Creativity' from 'Understanding Media', *ibid.*, p. 740.

[12] Thomas Miessgang, 'Kiki Kogelnik', Angela Stief (ed.), *POWER UP – Female Pop Art*, Kunsthalle Wien/ Dumont, Vienna, 2010, p. 185.

[13] Hal Foster, *op.cit.*, p. 7.

Lest the critical aspect of Kogelnik's work go unnoticed – as can happen given her exuberant palette – the repetition of skulls and skeletons attests to her association of annihilation with technological progress. From the earliest drawings like *Untitled (Skeleton)* (1957) and *Untitled (Tod mit Schürze)* (1958) through to exuberant paintings such as *Death With Sunglasses* (c. 1963), later hangings like *Nobody Loves Me* (1970) and the ceramic sculpture *Hungriger Totenkopf* (c. 1986), Kogelnik remained fascinated by mortality and peppered her work with macabre memento mori. This stripping back of the body to its bare bones offered Kogelnik a means of depicting a genderless body and it is true, too, that the sex of the more corporeal figures in her hangings and space paintings is left deliberately ambiguous. While Kogelnik's work adopted the iconography of the feminist movement in a more overt manner in the next decade, her works from the 1960s propose a radical vision of the future, especially when viewed in the context of the widespread objectification of the female form at the time. These works entail the re-imagination of the body itself, dissolved of male/female difference and freed from the weight of sexual politics.

As this text established from the beginning, Kogelnik is often classified as a Pop artist. Terms such as these are a helpful shorthand when attempting to contextualise an artist for a new audience, but labels can also be limiting. While the ambivalence of Pop art to the new products, technologies and politics of the commercial world is well known – Warhol's banality contrasting with the deadly seriousness of his subjects or Richard Hamilton's profession of both reverence and cynicism in equal measure, for example – it is true that artists on the periphery of that movement, like Kogelnik, sounded a more overtly cautious note, making work that was both more personal in approach and more idiosyncratic in terms of form and execution. With her extraordinary visual language and her insightful depictions of humanity in a technological age, Kogelnik's work eludes categorisation and exceeds our expectations of what Pop art can be.

Ciara Moloney

Claes, c. 1970
Sheet vinyl with chromed steel hanger
143.2 × 57.2 × 4.5 cm

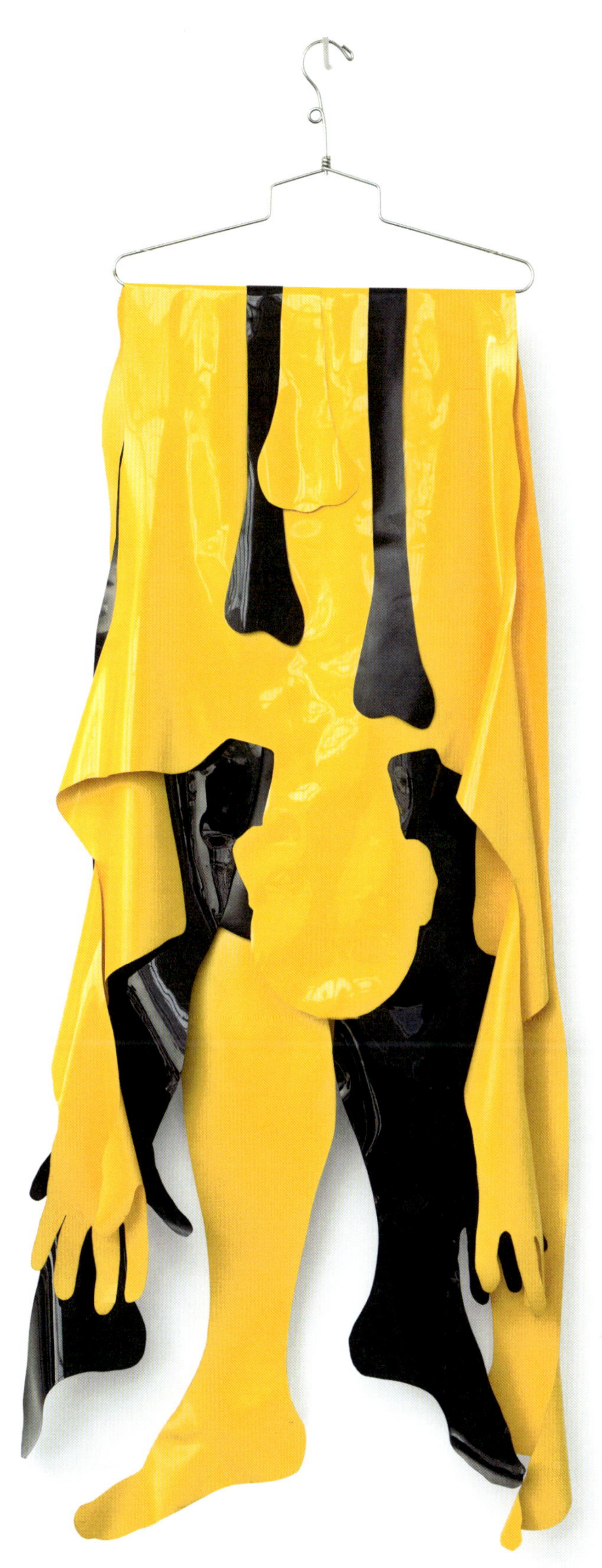

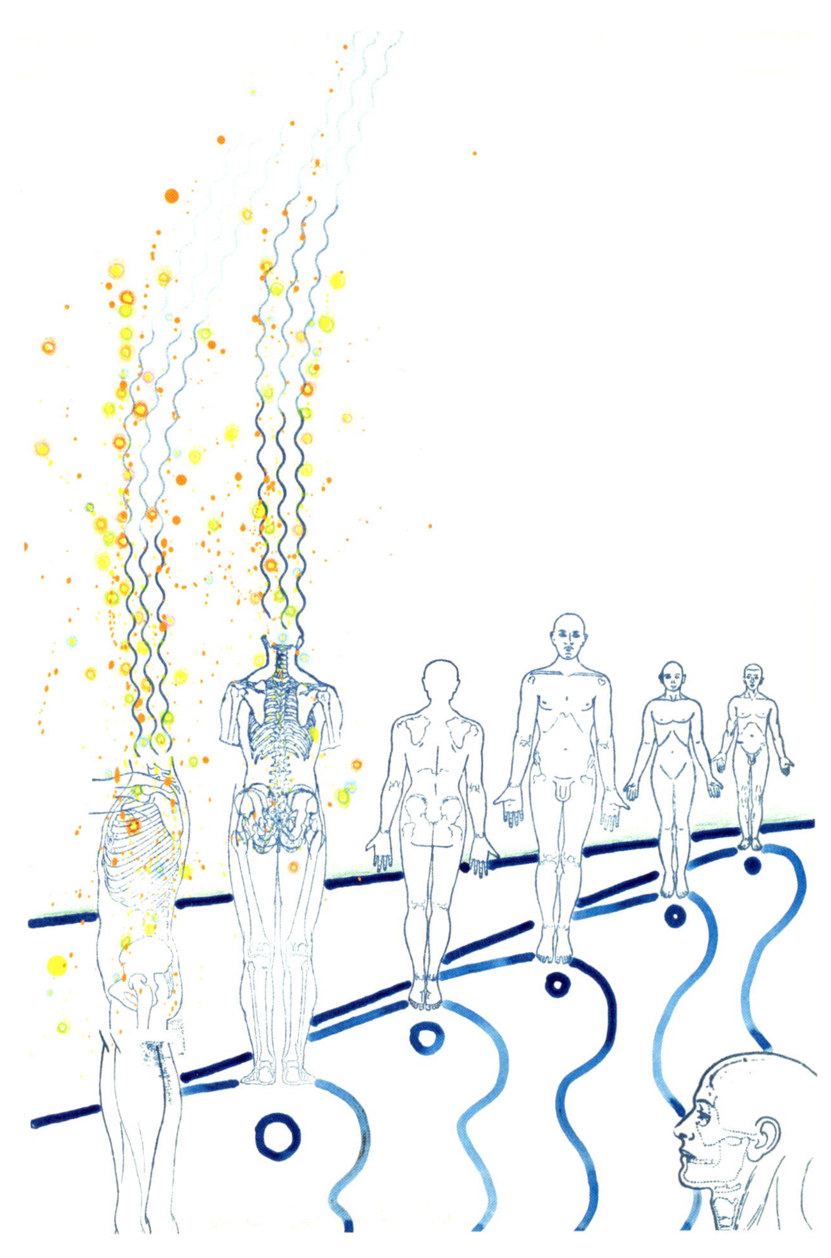

Robots, 1966
Ink and colour pencil on paper
56.2 × 38 cm

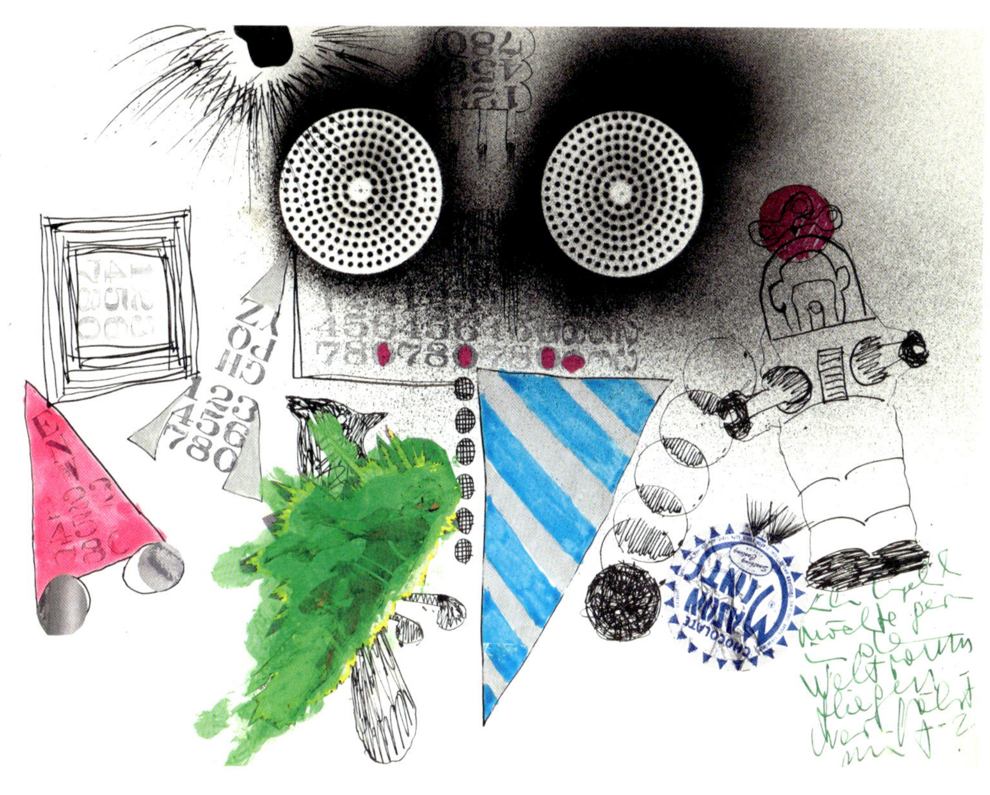

Untitled (Space), c. 1963
Acrylic, enamel, India ink, ink and foil wrapper on paper
35.5 × 55.5 cm

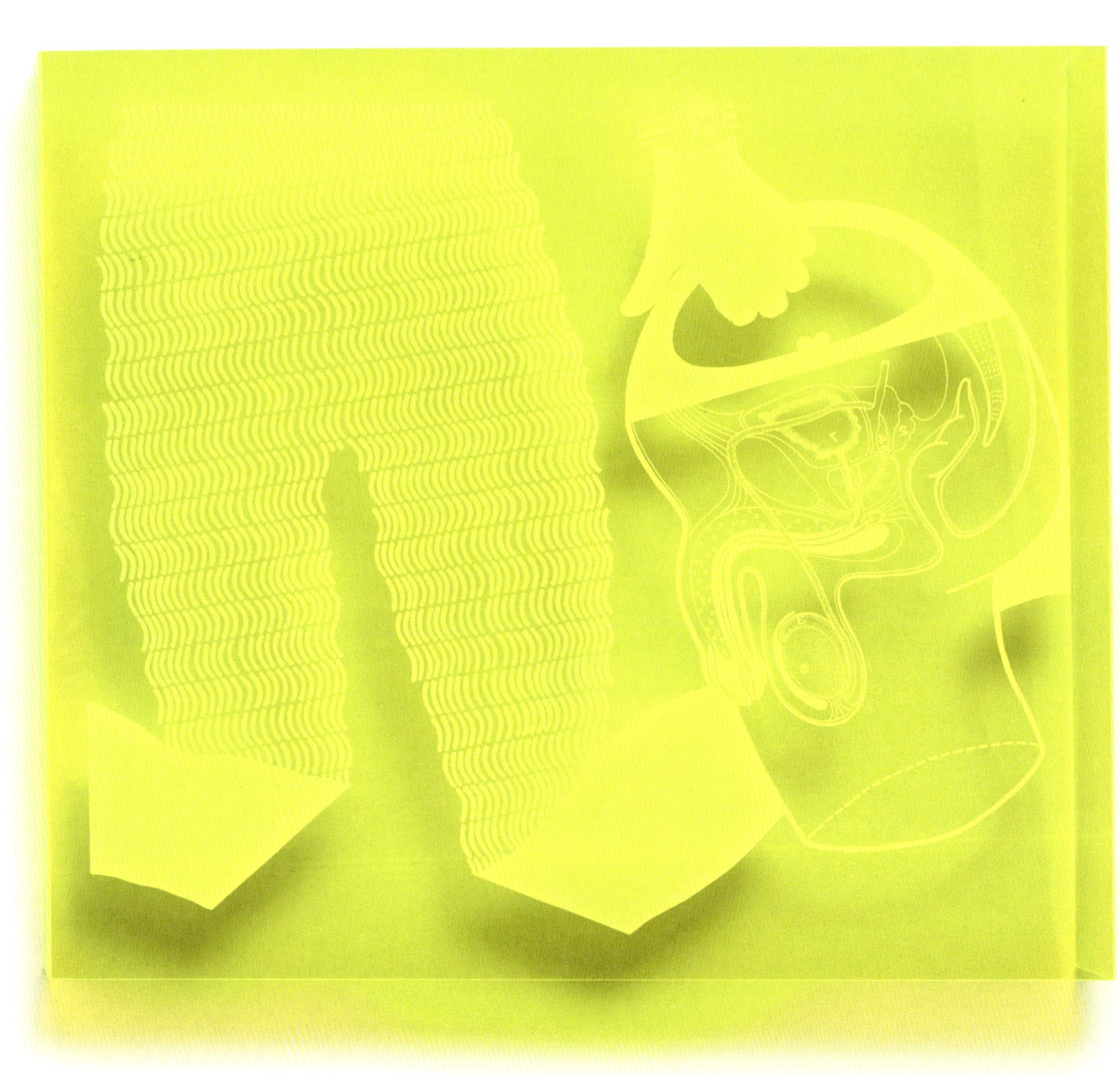

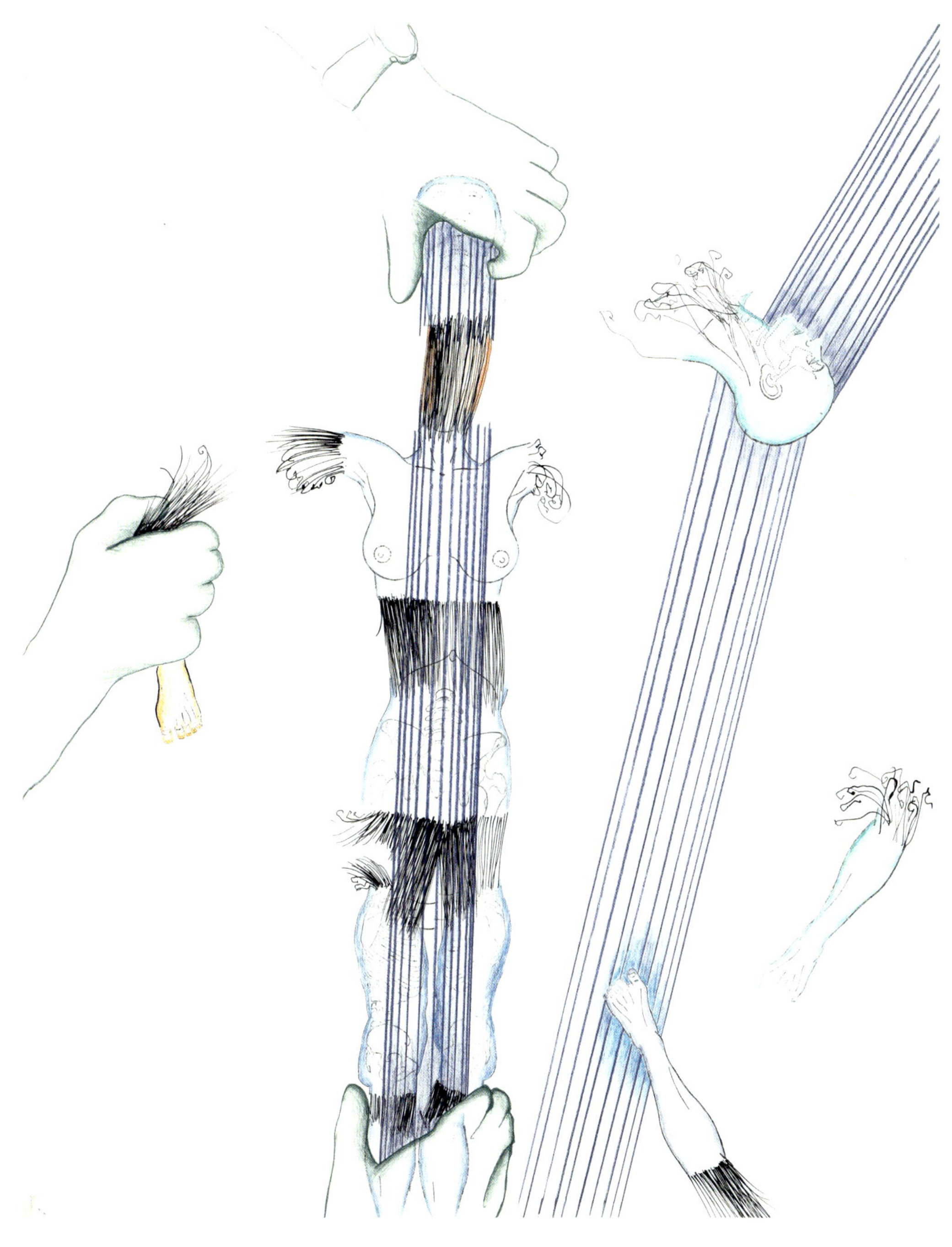

Untitled (Flight), 1968
Silkscreen on Plexiglas
64 × 76.7 × 5.4 cm

Robots, 1966
India ink, ink and colour pencil on paper
73.5 × 58.5 cm

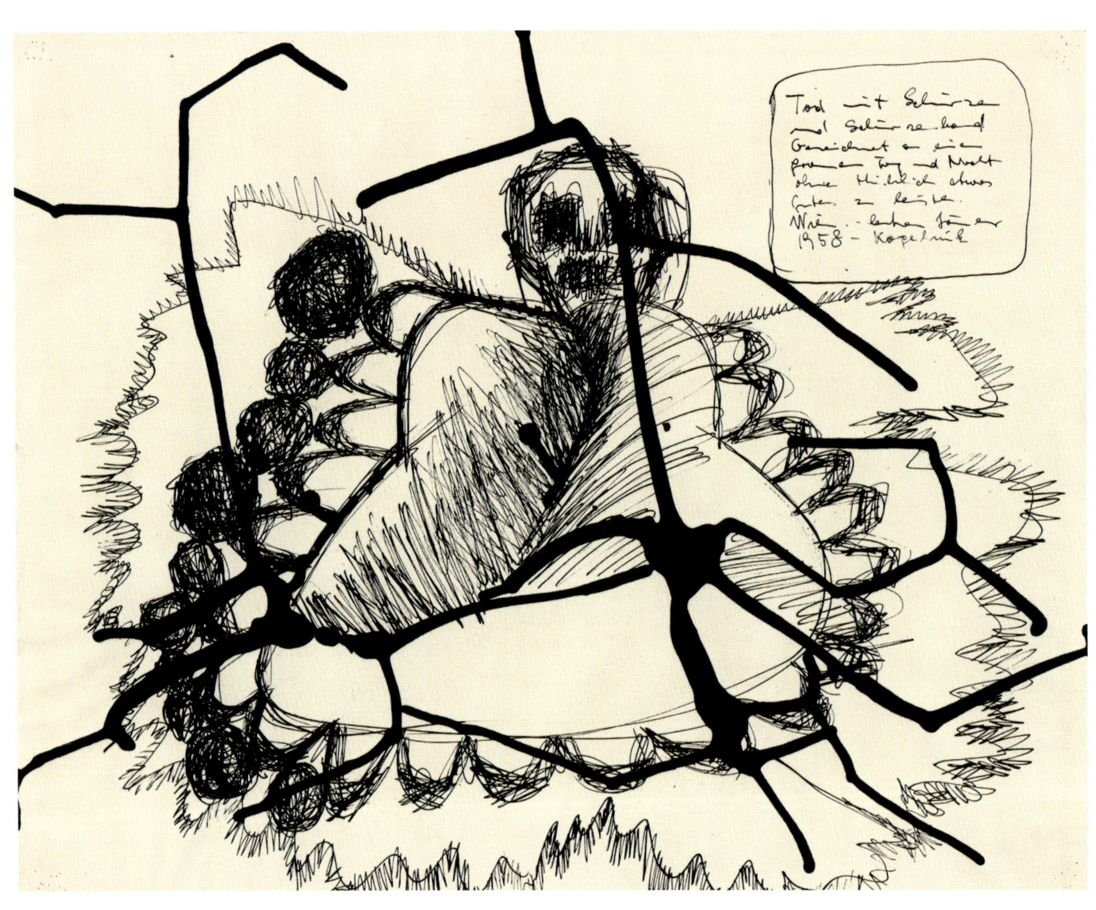

Untitled (Tod mit Schürze), 1958
India ink on paper
40.2 × 51 cm

Mono, c. 1970
Sheet vinyl, chromed steel hangers and rolling garment rack
124.3 × 84.5 × 57.5 cm

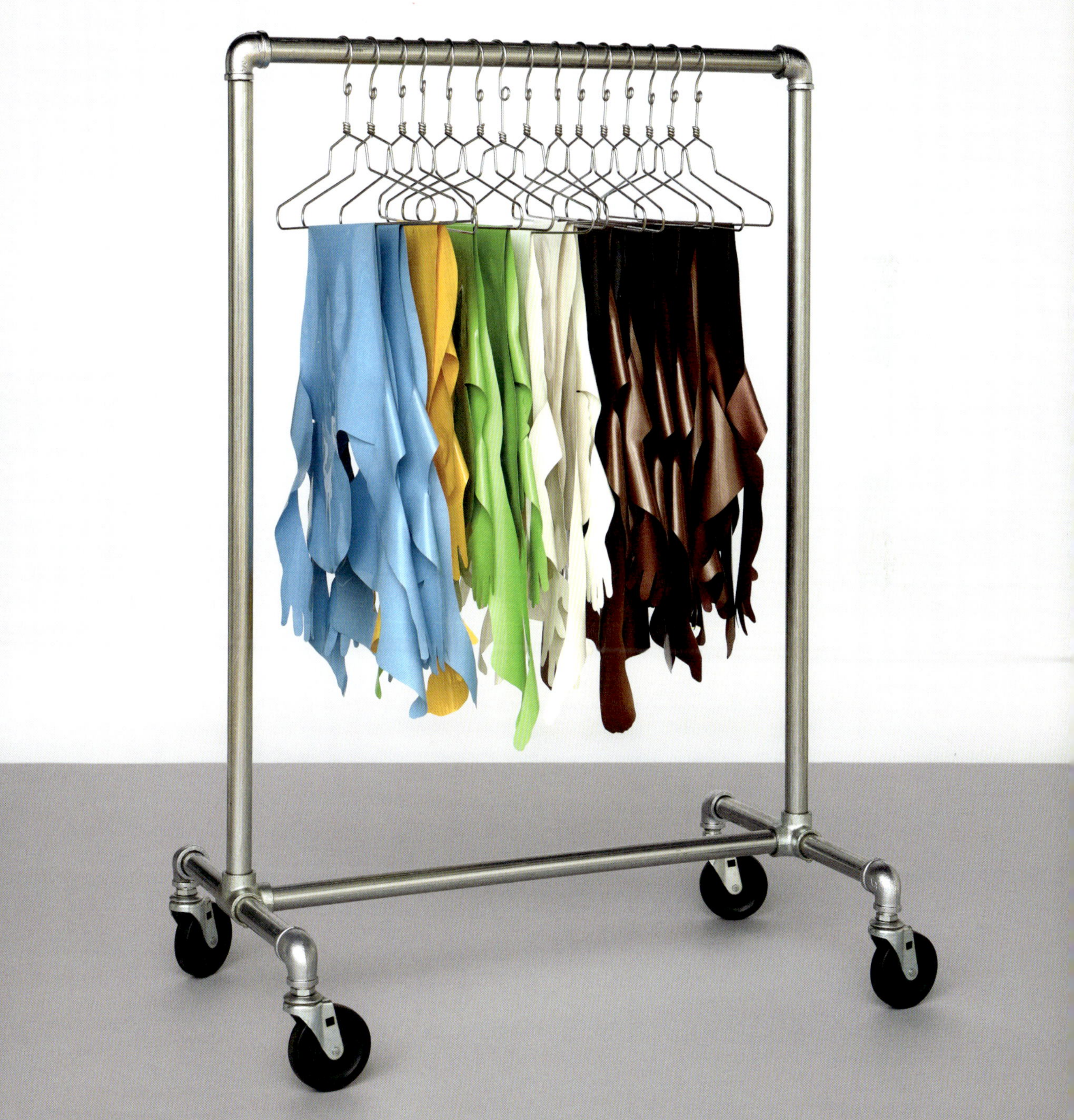

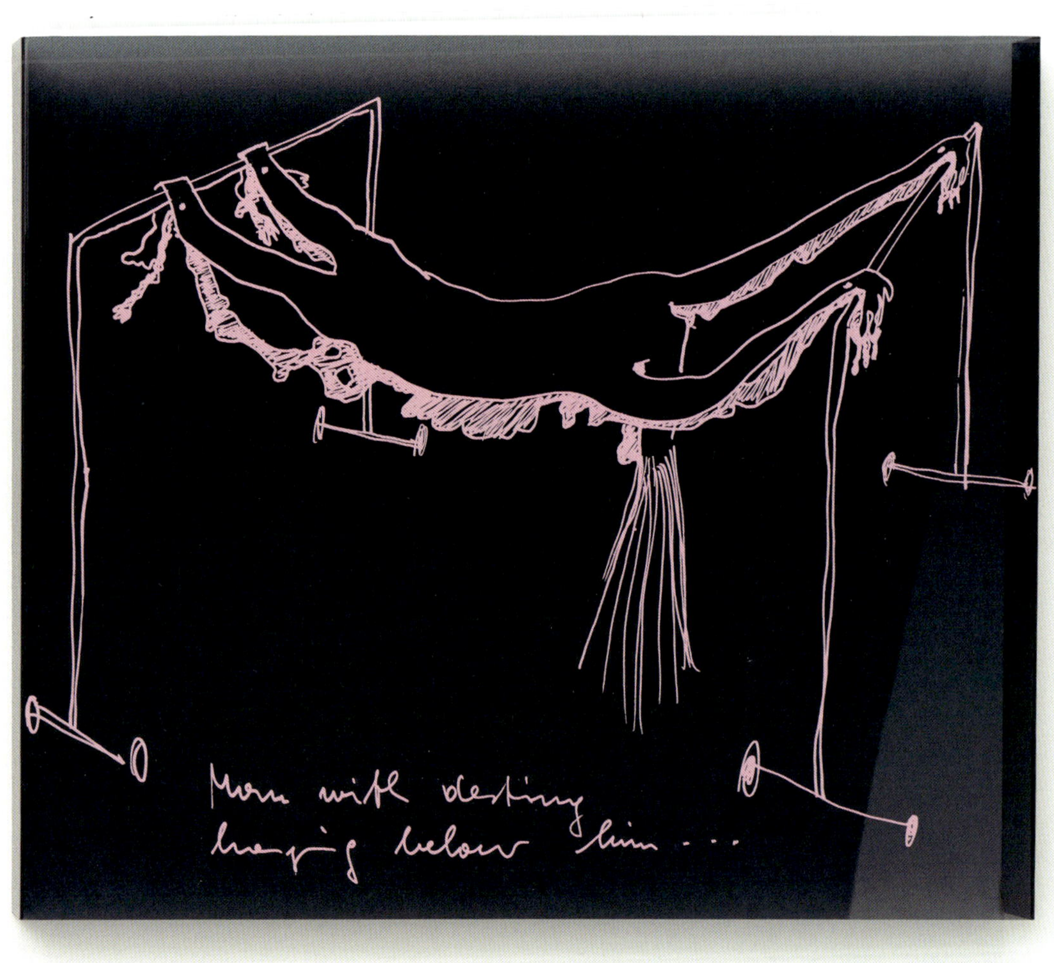

Untitled (Man with destiny), 1970
Silkscreen on Plexiglas
64 × 76.7 × 5.4 cm

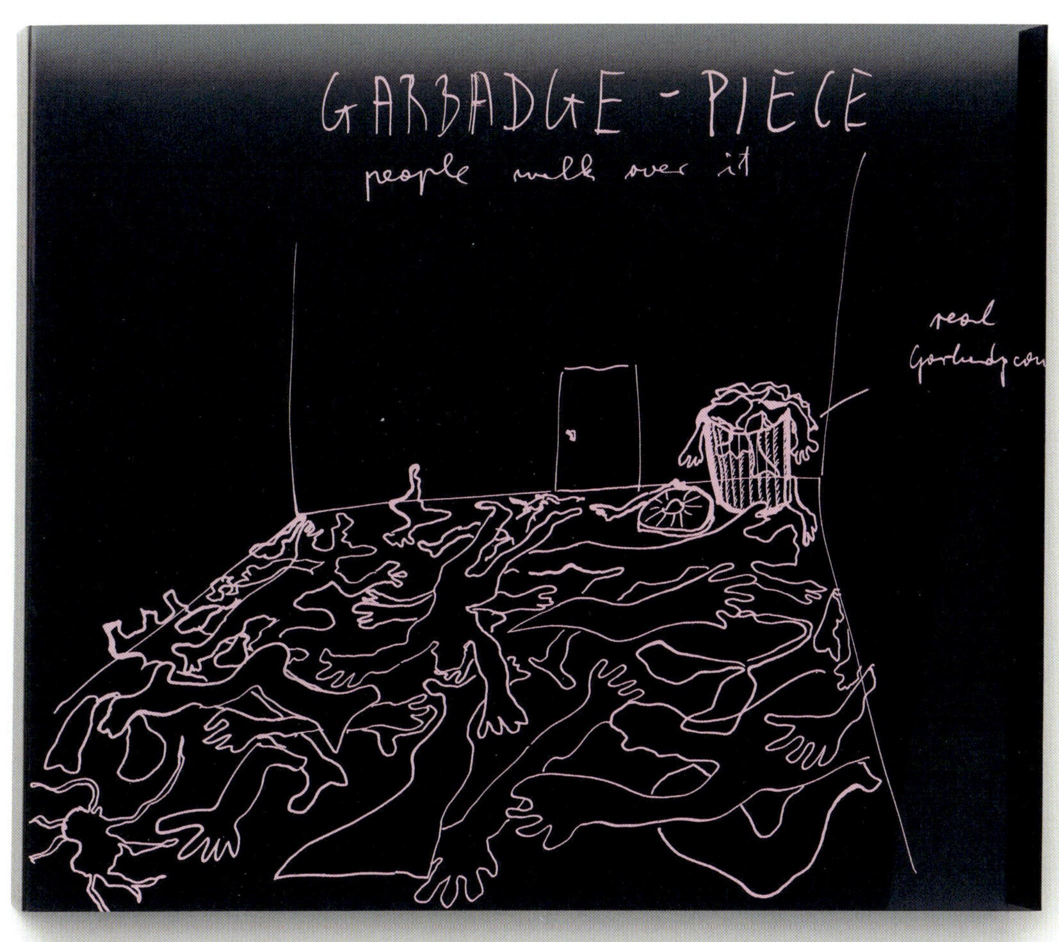

Untitled (Garbage piece), 1970
Silkscreen on Plexiglas
64 × 76.7 × 5.4 cm

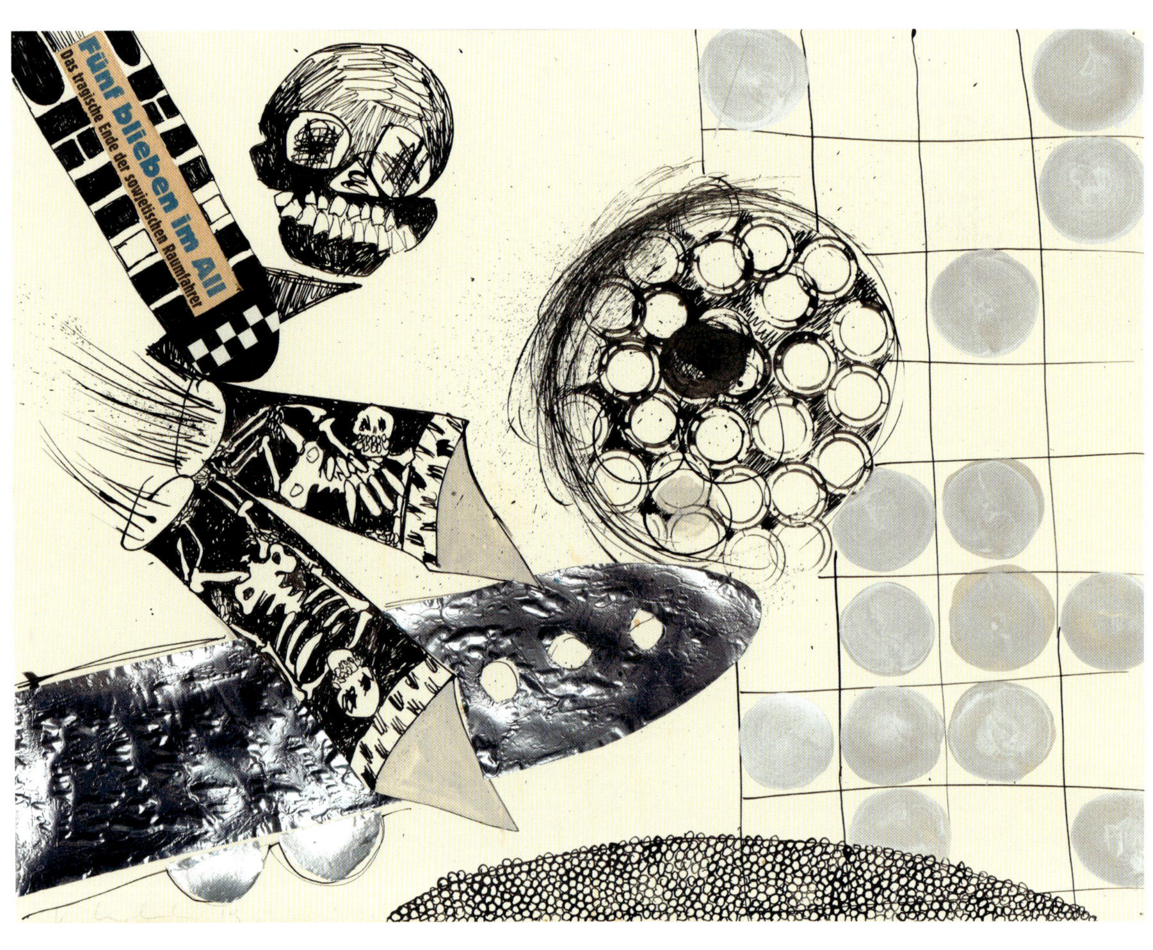

Space, 1963
Acrylic, India ink, foil and collage on paper
50 × 65 cm

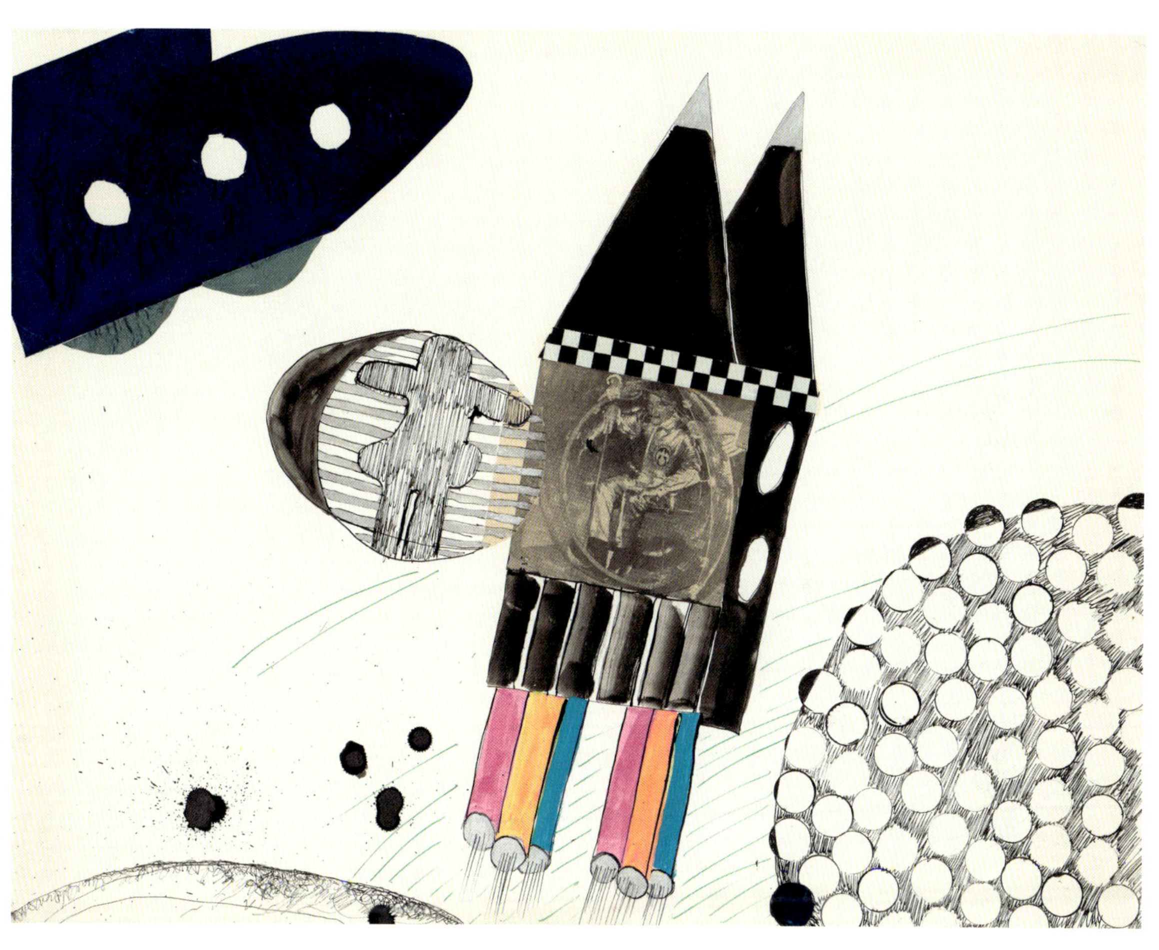

Untitled (Spaceship), c. 1963
Acrylic, India ink, ink, foil and collage on paper
50 × 65 cm

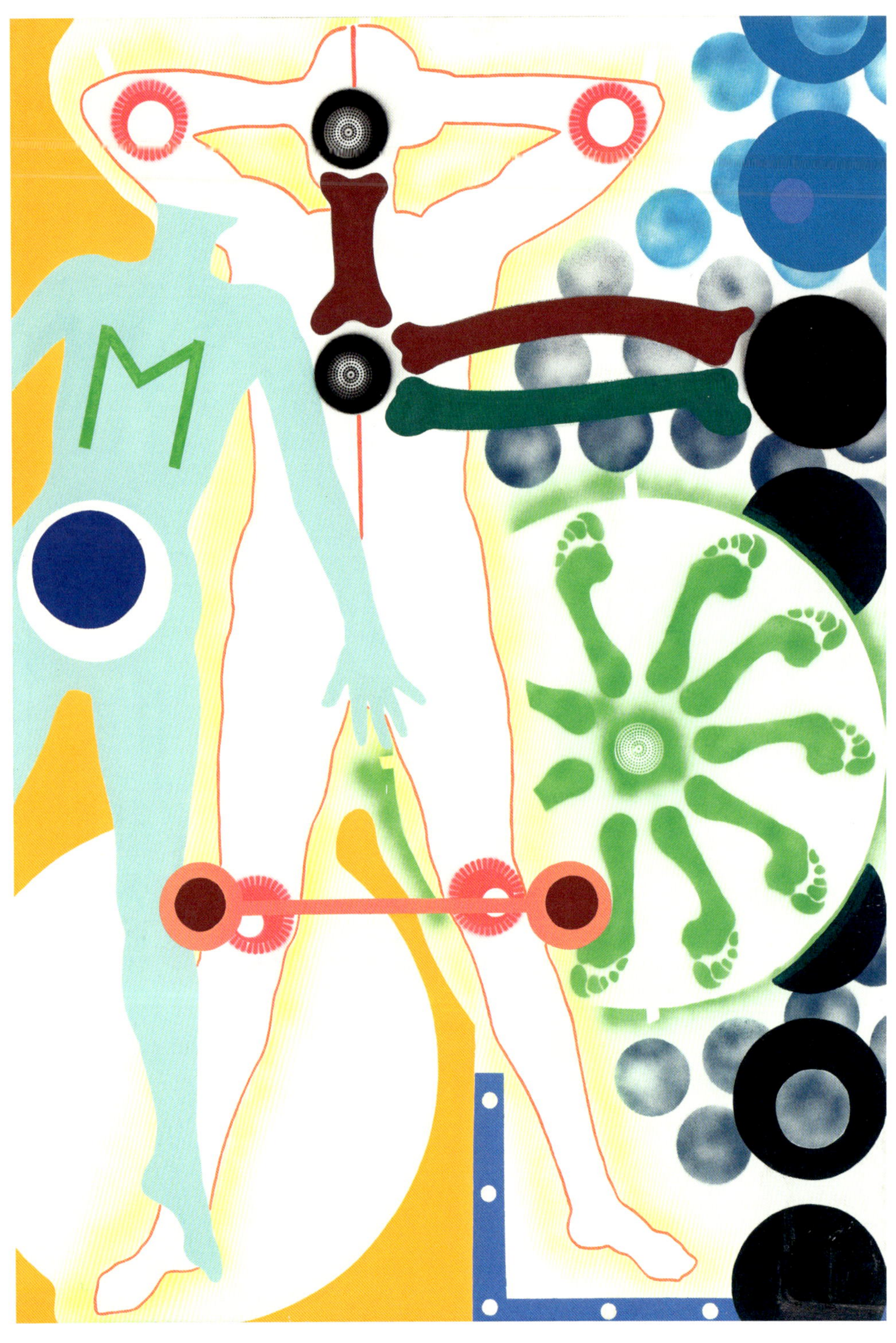

Untitled (M), c. 1964
Oil and acrylic on canvas
203 × 142.7 cm

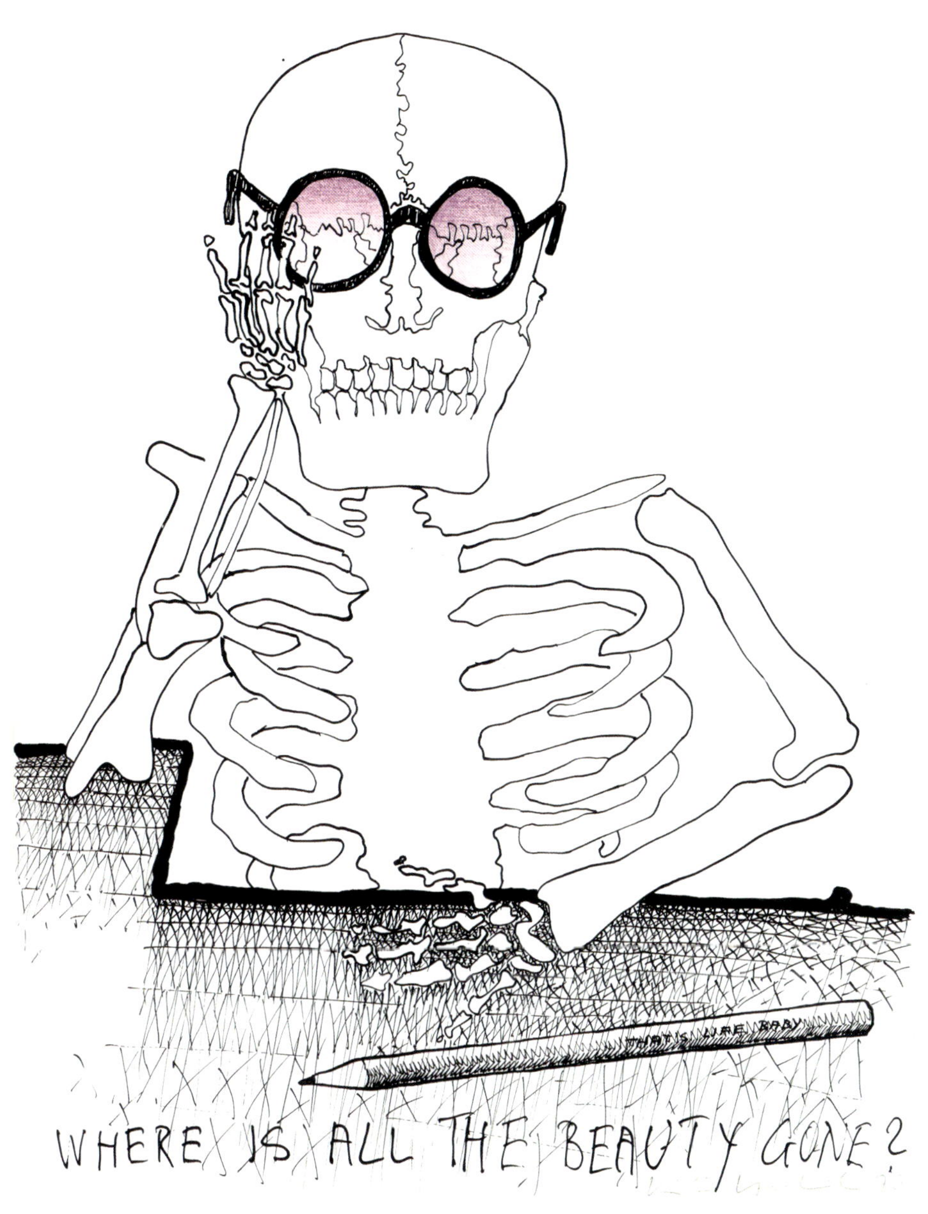

Where is All the Beauty Gone?, 1970
India ink and colour pencil on paper
34.9 × 28 cm

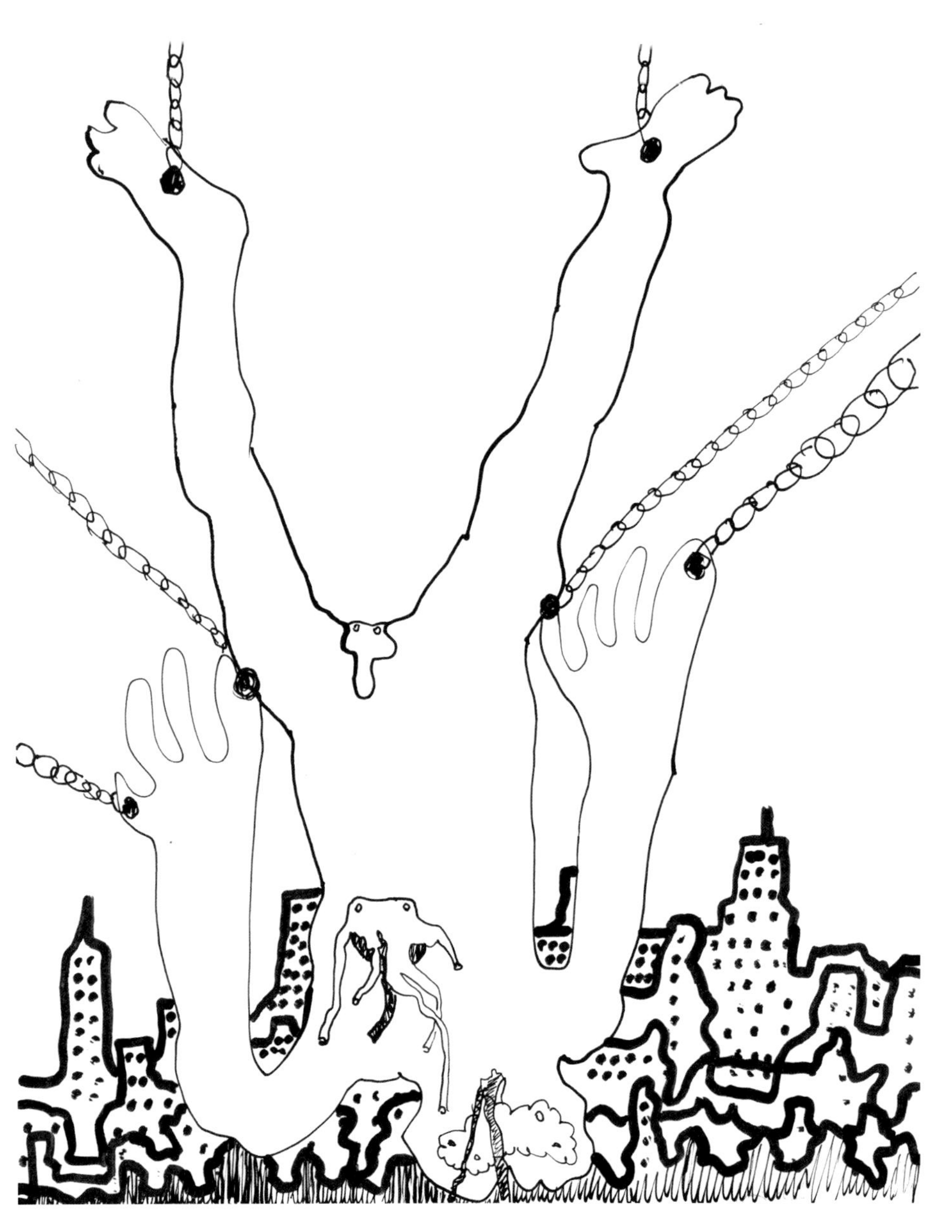

Untitled (Hanging), 1970
India ink on paper
35 × 28 cm

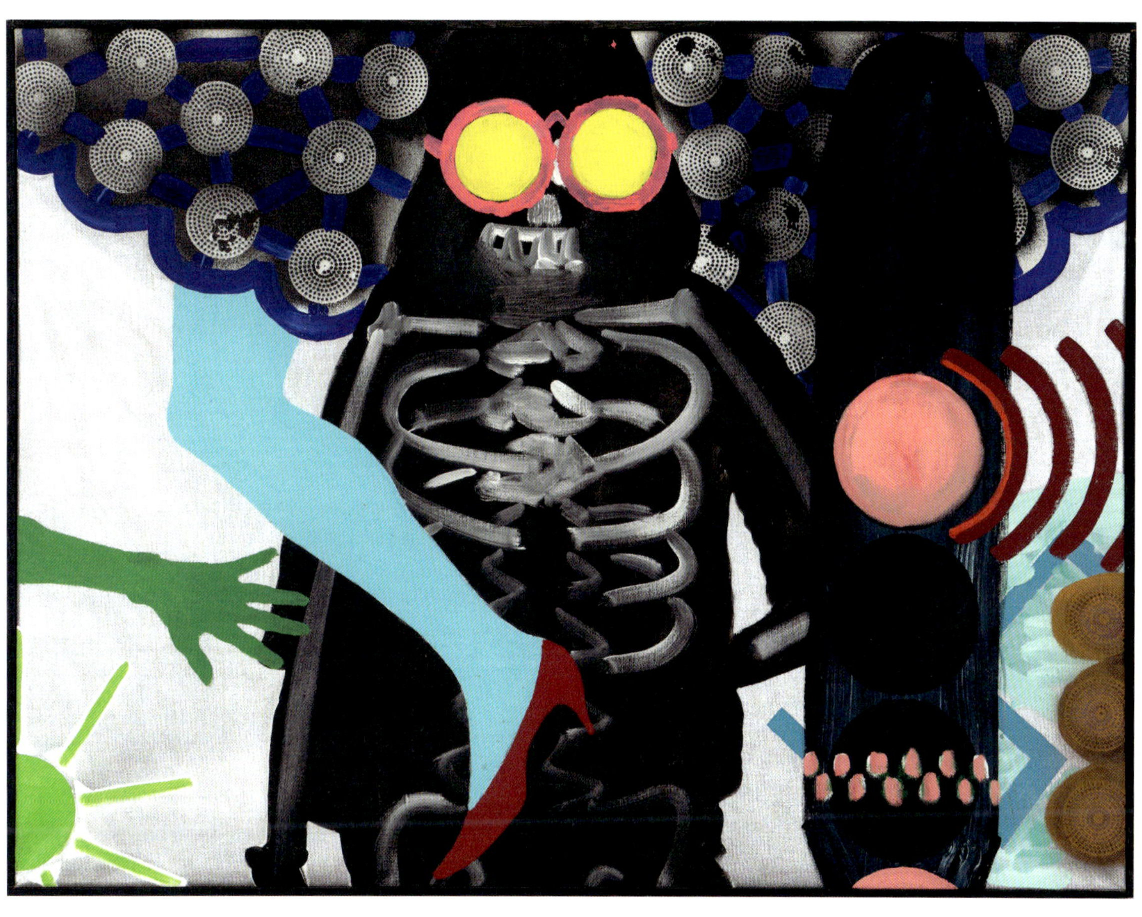

Death With Sunglasses, c.1963
Oil and acrylic on canvas
91.2 × 121.5 cm

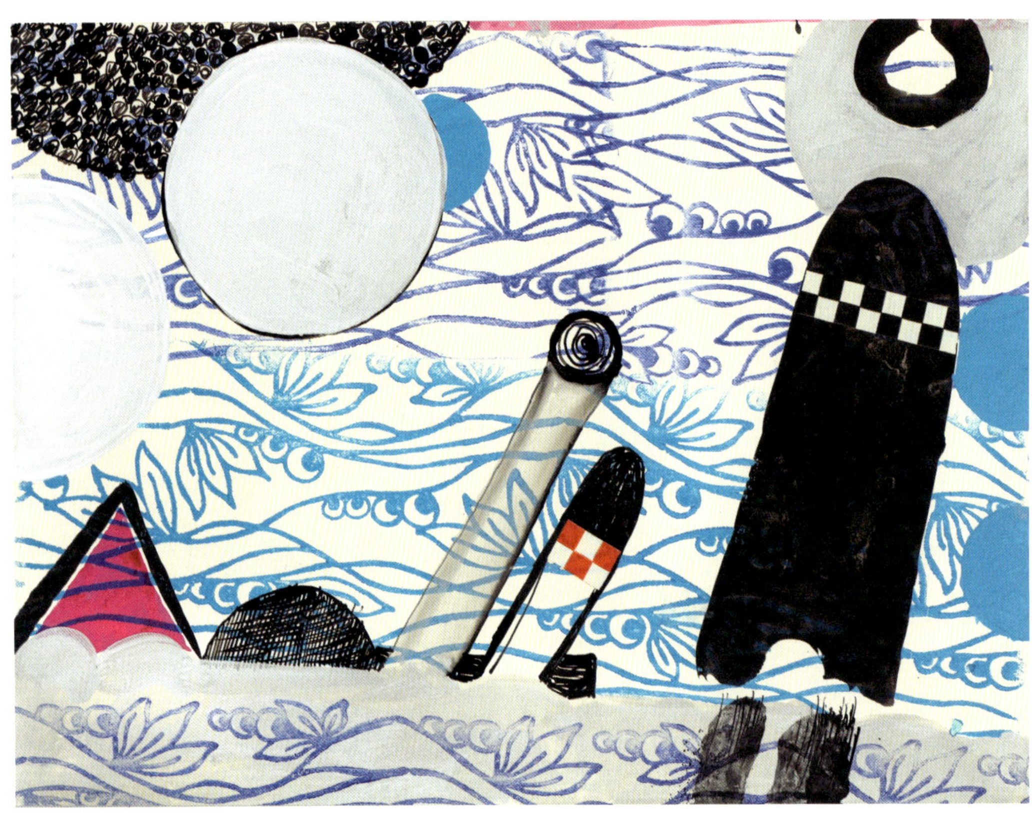

Untitled (Spaceship), c.1963
Acrylic, India ink and colour pencil on paper
21.3 × 29.4 cm

Nobody Loves Me, 1970
Sheet vinyl, wire hanger and acrylic on wood
41 × 30.6 × 15.8 cm

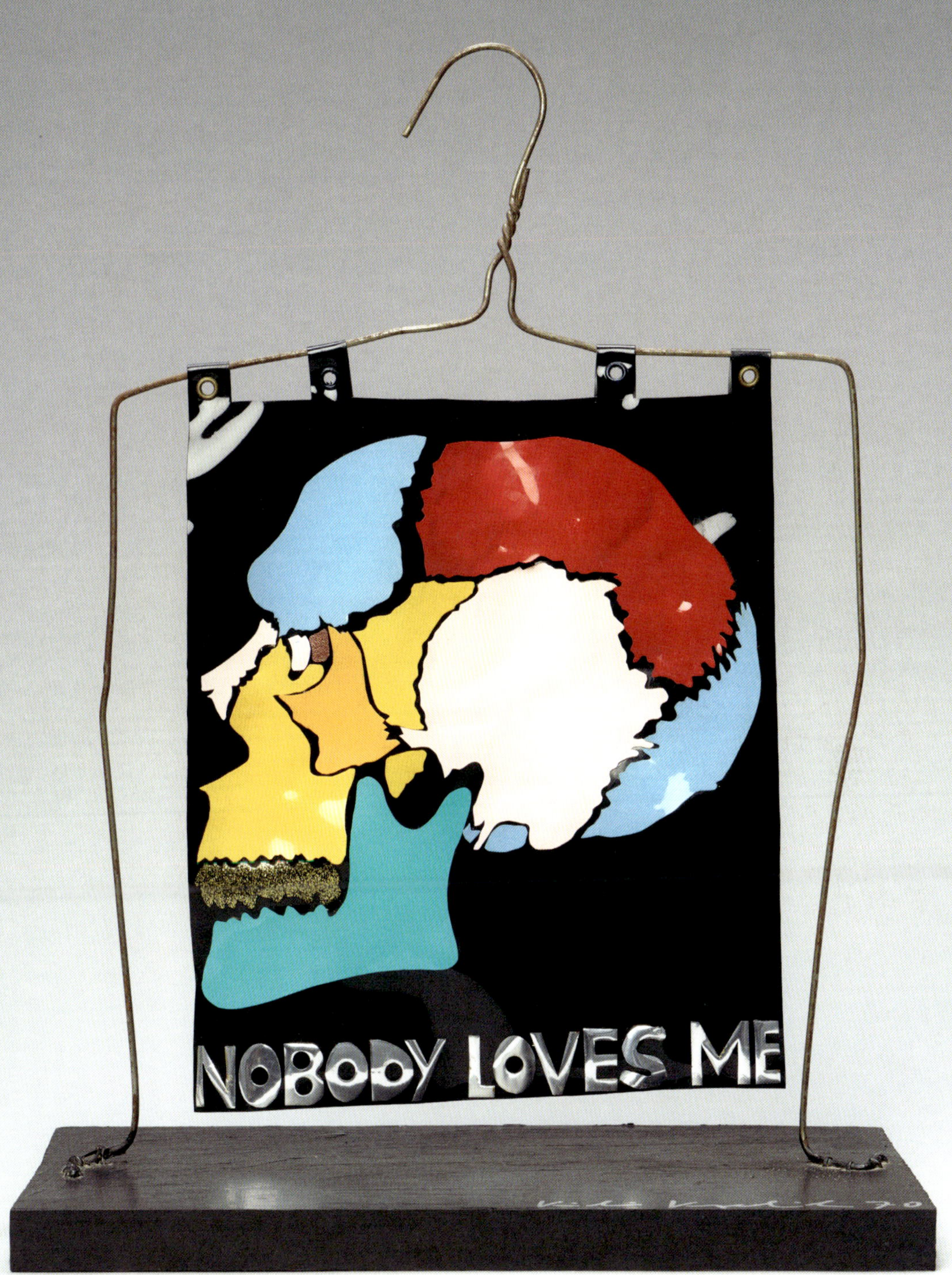

NOBODY LOVES ME

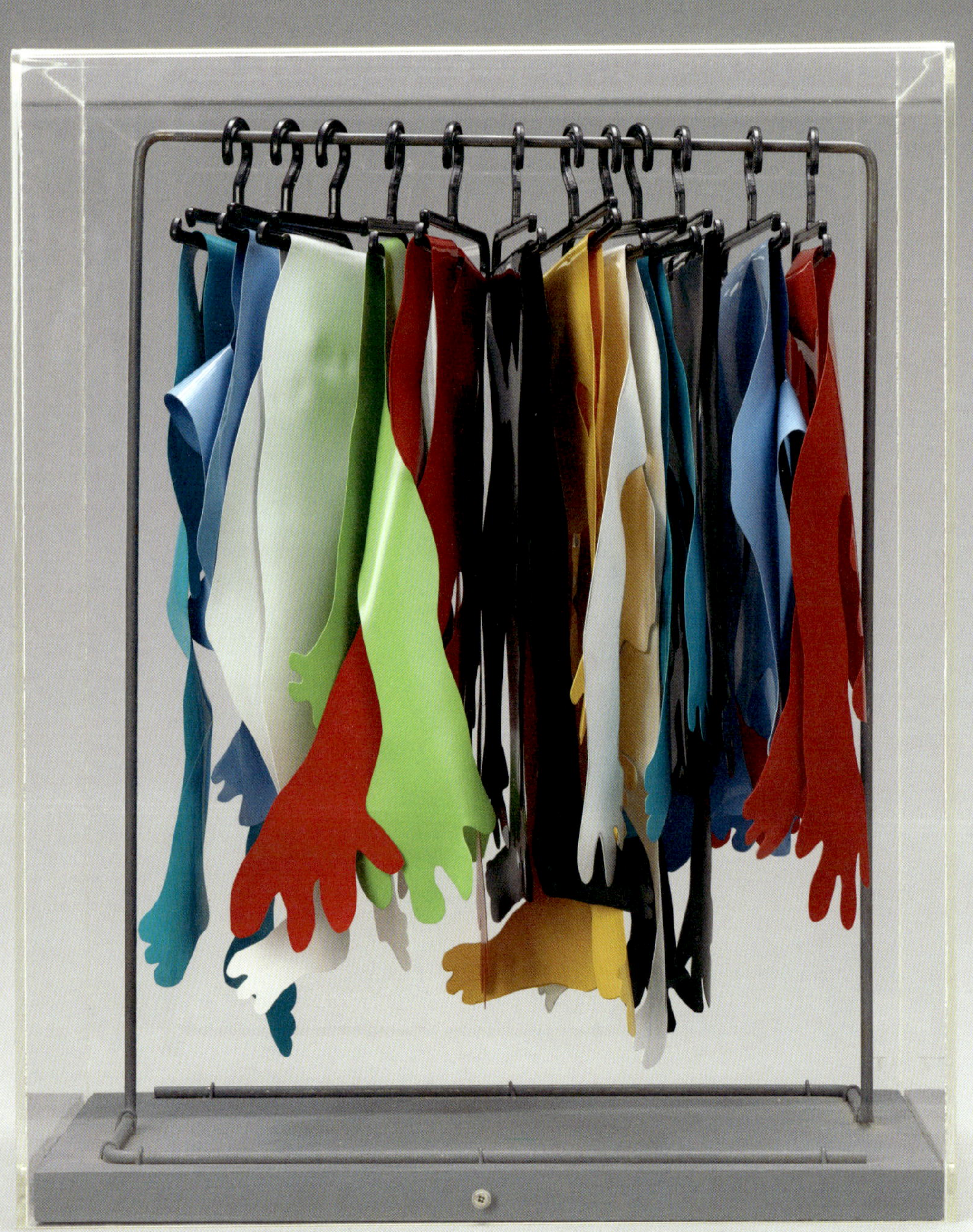

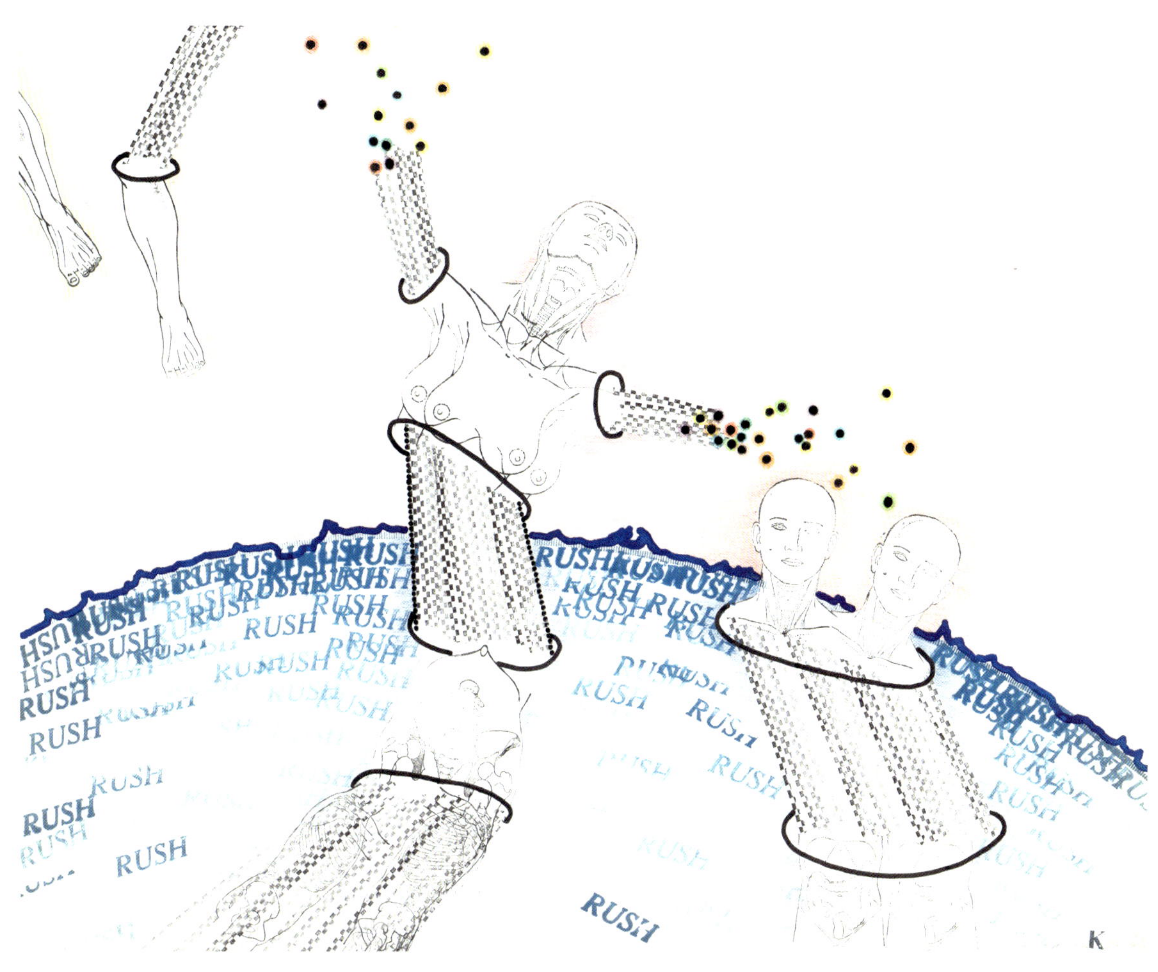

Small Seventh Ave People, 1970–93
Sheet vinyl, acrylic hangers, Plexiglas, steel and acrylic on wood
45.3 × 37.3 × 20.5 cm

Robots, 1966
India ink, ink and colour pencil on paper
58.9 × 73.5 cm

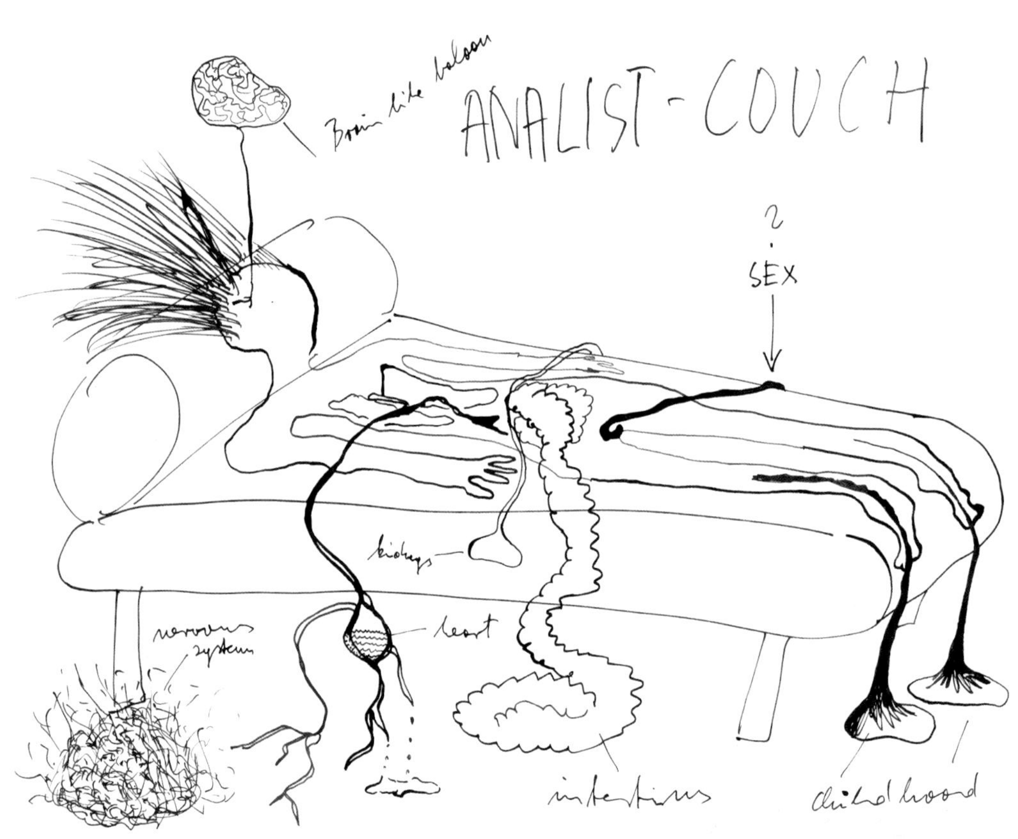

Analyst Couch, 1970
India ink on paper
35.3 × 43 cm

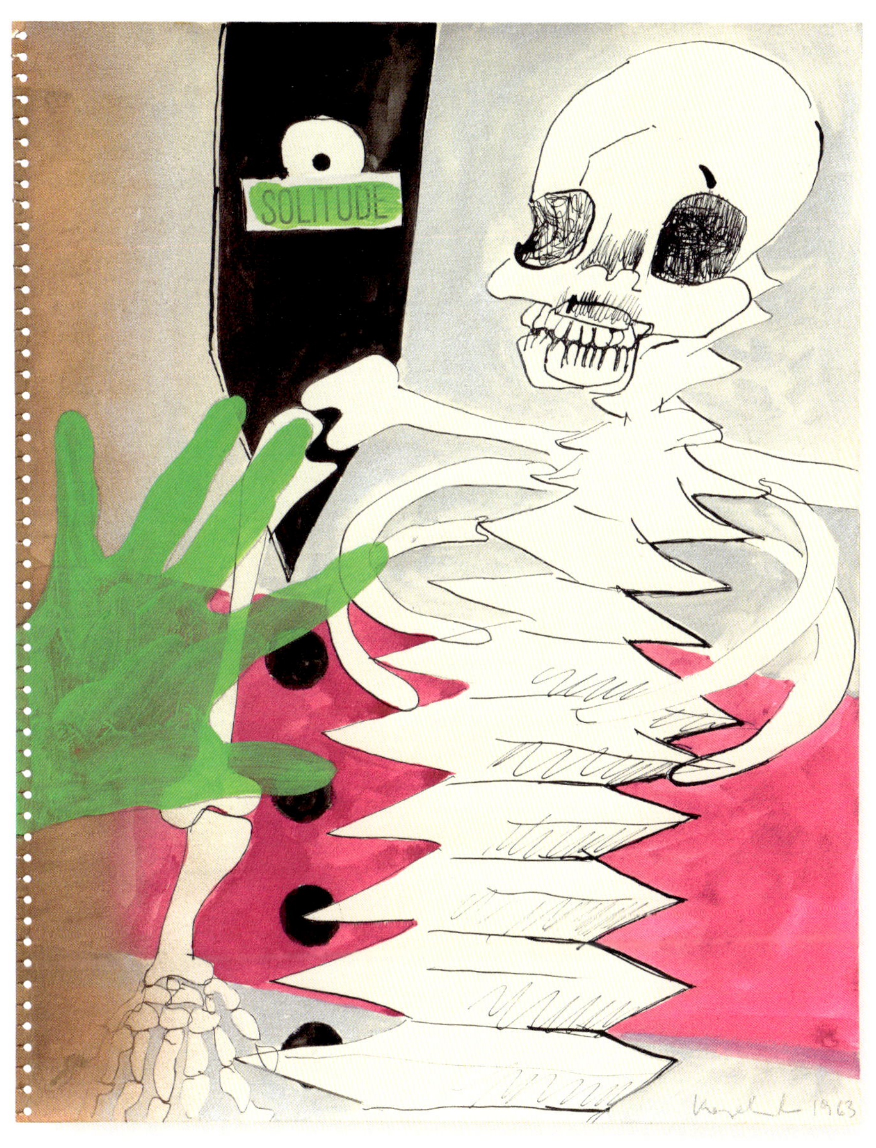

Untitled (Solitude), 1963
Acrylic, India ink, watercolour and collage on paper
41.7 × 33 cm

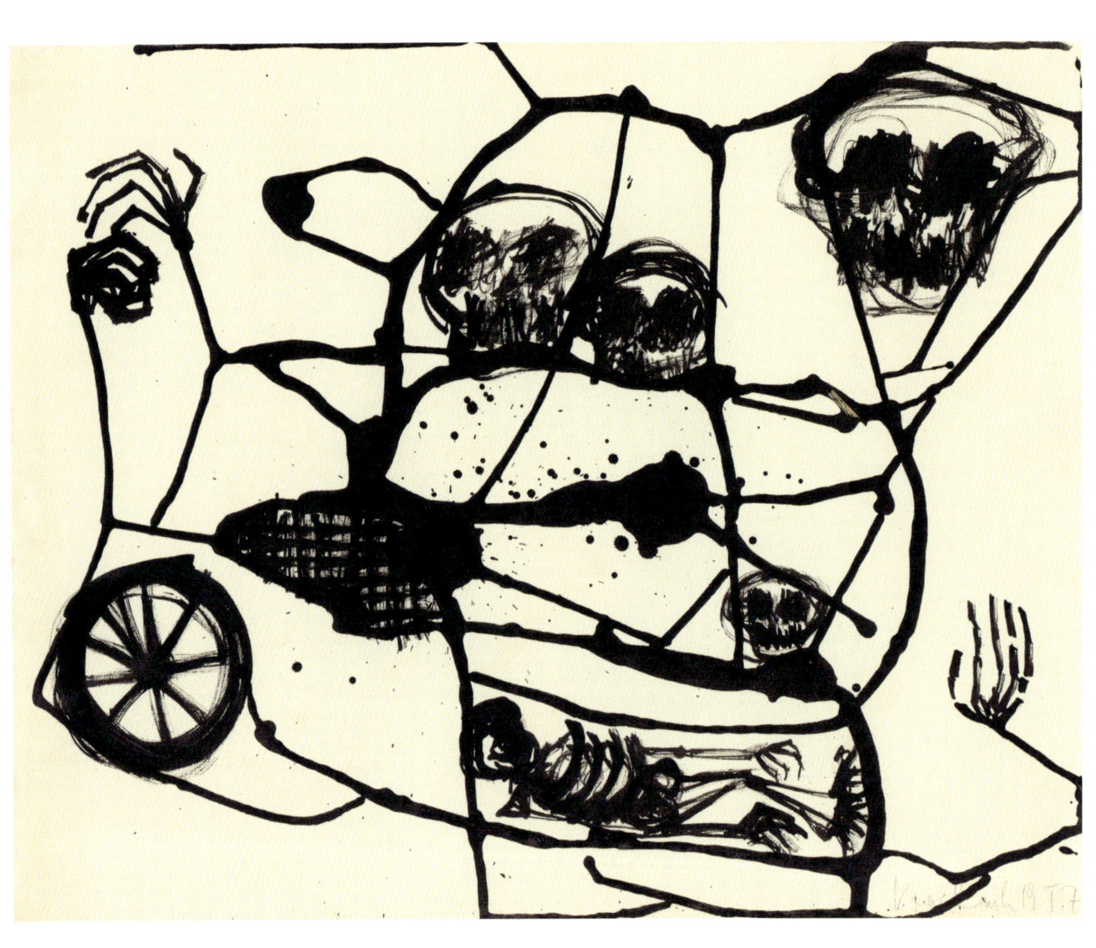

Untitled (Skeleton), 1957
India ink on paper
40.3 × 51 cm

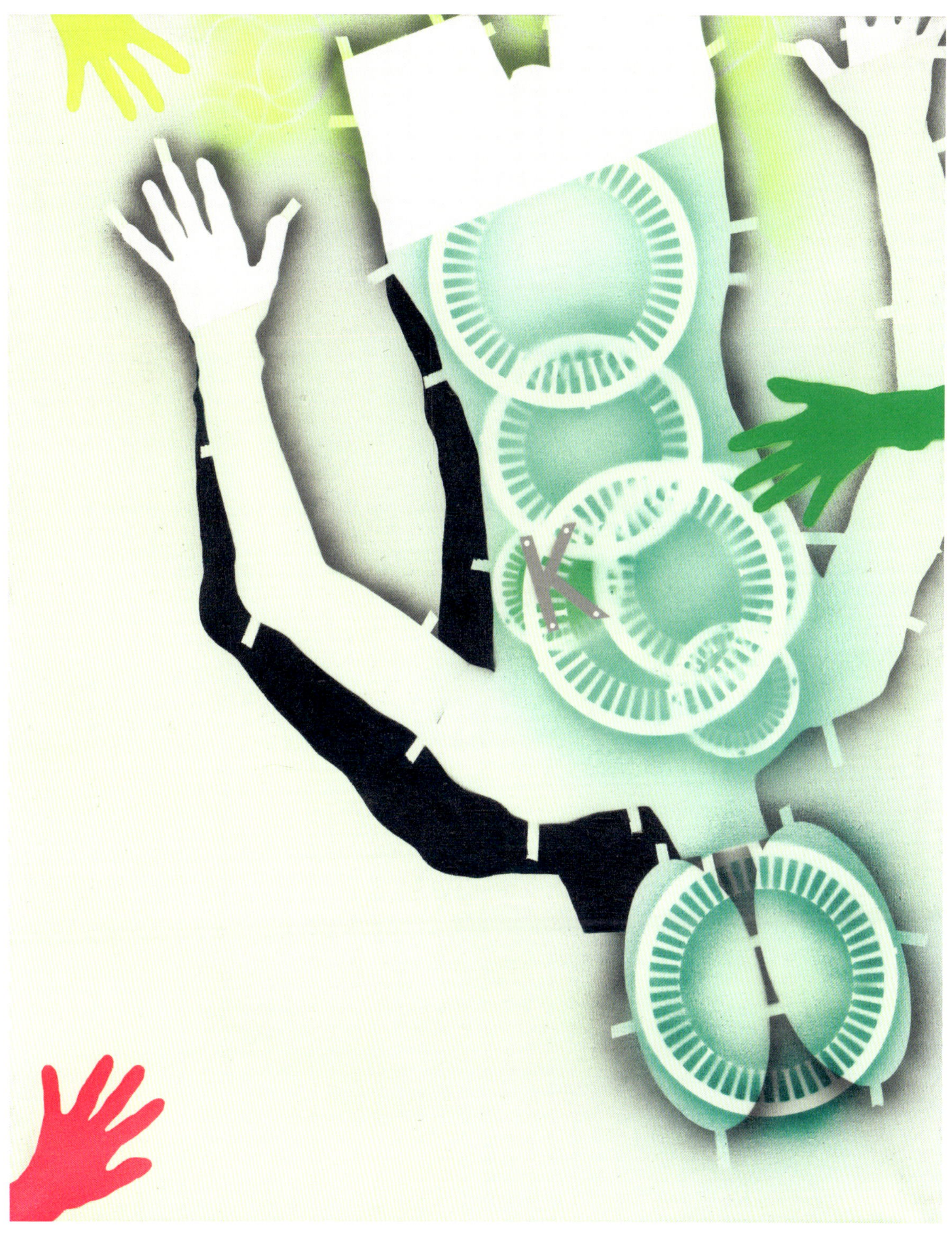

Ikarus, 1965
Oil and acrylic on canvas
128.9 × 104.2 cm

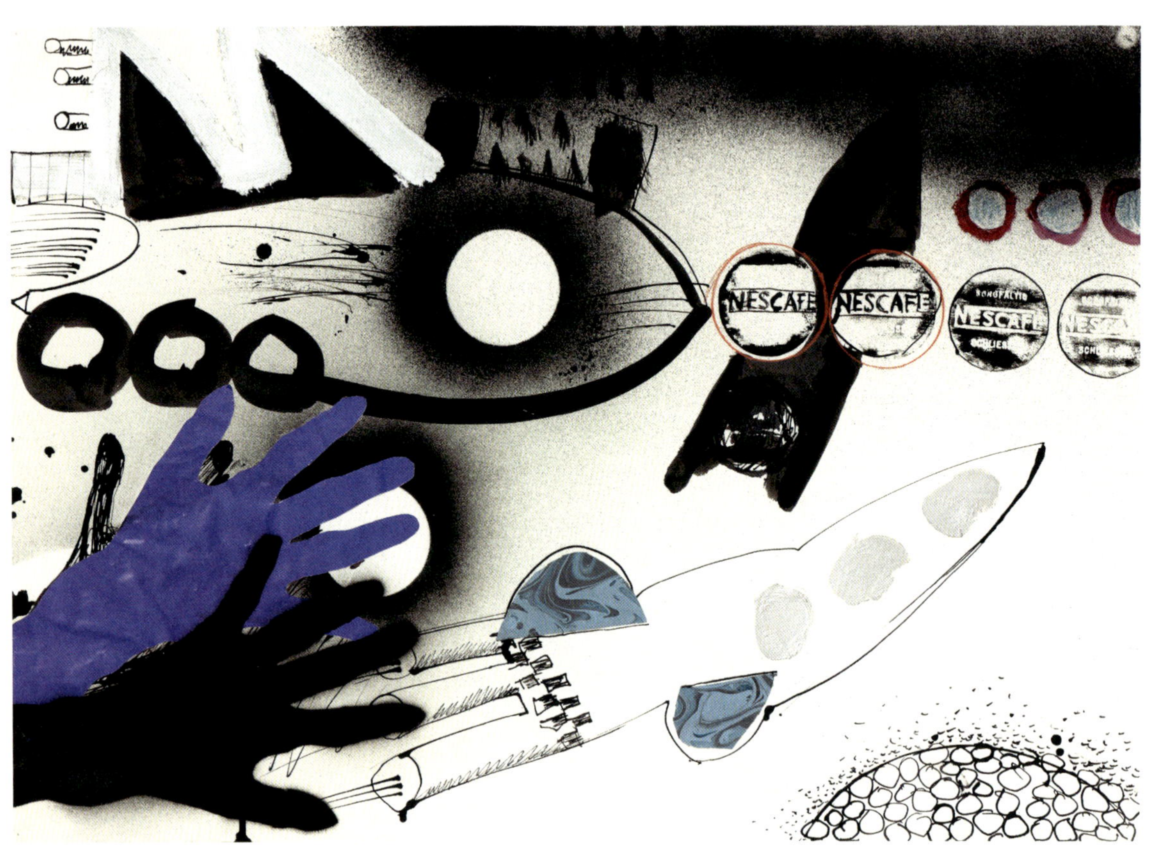

Untitled (Nescafe Nescafe), c.1963
Acrylic, enamel, India ink, colour pencil, foil and collage on paper
44 × 62.8 cm

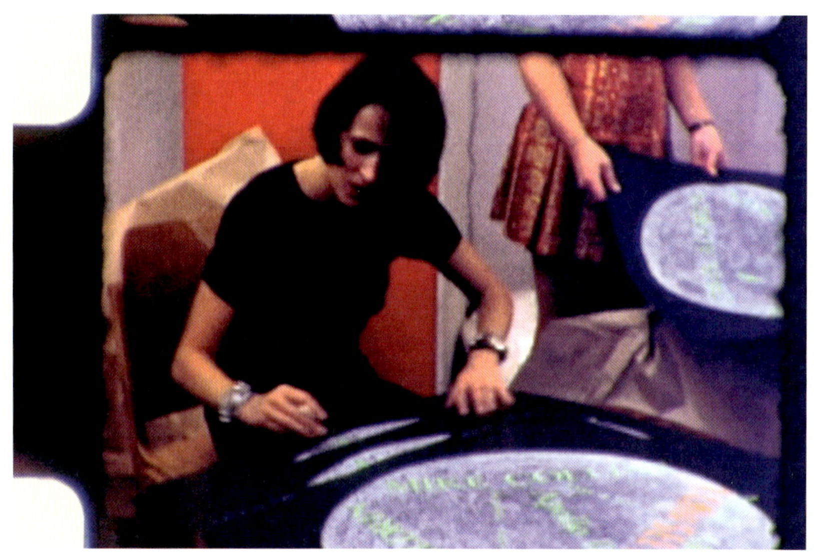

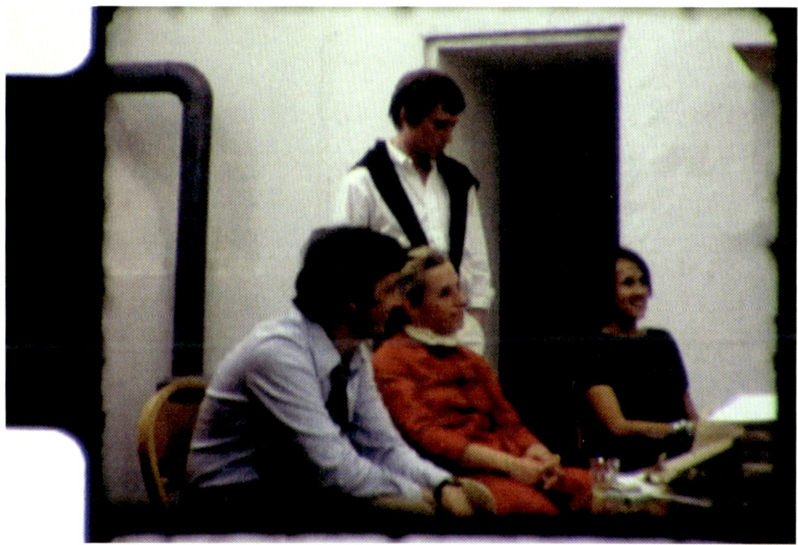

Documentation of *Moonhappening*, 1969
8mm colour film
12:30 min

Published by Modern Art Oxford on the occasion
of the exhibition

Kiki Kogelnik: Fly Me to the Moon
22 August – 18 October 2015

Modern Art Oxford
30 Pembroke Street
Oxford OX1 1BP
United Kingdom
+44 (0) 1865 722733
modernartoxford.org.uk

Programme team:
Ciara Moloney, Emma Ridgway, Ben Roberts,
Sally Shaw, Paul Teigh, Seb Thomas,
Jonathan Weston

Publication edited by Ciara Moloney
Editorial assistance by Jonathan Weston
Copy edited by Eileen Daly
Project Management by Pilar Zevallos
Design by Anaïs Horn and Alexander Nussbaumer
Printed in edition of 1,000

© Modern Art Oxford and the authors, 2015

ISBN: 978-1-901352-64-1
A catalogue record for this book is available from the
British Library

Museum of Modern Art Limited
Registered charity no. 313035

Image credits:
All images © 2015
Kiki Kogelnik Foundation Vienna / New York

All images by Andrew Rinkhy, except for pp. 13, 37
and 51 by Lisa Rastl.

Modern Art Oxford is grateful to the many individuals,
companies and organisations that have helped to
realise *Kiki Kogelnik: Fly Me to the Moon.*

With special thanks to Mono Schwarz-Kogelnik,
Dr George Schwarz, Pilar Zevallos and Katya Taneva
from the Kiki Kogelnik Foundation, Elisabeth Koegler,
Director, Austrian Cultural Forum London, Andrew
Rinkhy and Simone Subal Gallery, New York.

Kiki Kogelnik: Fly Me to the Moon is supported by the
Kiki Kogelnik Foundation and Bundeskanzleramt
Österreich

Modern Art Oxford is supported by Oxford City
Council and Arts Council England

With thanks to Modern Art Oxford's Patrons and
Director's Circle Members

Council of Management:
David Issac (Chair), Heidi Baravalle, Hussein Barma,
Diana Parker, Amanda Poole, Robert Rickman,
Tania Rotherwick, Andy Verschoyle

Modern Art Oxford staff:
Ruba Asfahani, Communications Manager
Mohamed Bushara, Visitor Assistant
Lusiana Castiglione, Visitor Assistant
Laura Catsellis, Visitor Assistant
Andrew Charlwood, Visitor Assistant
Helen Corley, Development and Communications
Assistant
Jack Eden, Duty Manager
Sarah Ellingworth, Visitor Assistant
Lauren Greenaway, Visitor Assistant
Russell Harmon, Visitor Assistant
Simone Hesselberg, Visitor Assistant
Paul Hobson, Director
Jumana Hokan, Information and Bookings Assistant
Paulette Mae, Visitor Assistant
Deb Martindale, Visitor Assistant
Robert Mead, Visitor Assistant
Ciara Moloney, Curator of Exhibitions and Projects
Fennah Podschies, Head of Resources and
Enterprise
Hayley Raines, Executive Assistant and Project
Manager
Shona Ritchie, Shop Assistant
Emma Ridgway, Head of Programme (Maternity
Cover)
Ben Roberts, Curator of Education and Public
Programmes
Kay Sentance, Duty Manager
Sally Shaw, Head of Programme
Helen Shilton, Head of Operations and Visitor Services
Jamie Simmons, Visitor Assistant
Verity Slater, Director of Development and
Communications
Liz Smith, Development Manager
Lorraine Stone, Finance Manager
Paul Teigh, Production Manager
Seb Thomas, Assistant Gallery Manager
Jonathan Weston, Programme Coordinator
Charlotte White, Retail Manager
Joe Wilson, Duty Manager

Technical team:
Scot Blyth, Tom Cretton, Chris Jackson,
Perce Jerrom, Tom Milnes, Sean Reynard,
Russell Wainwright

MODERN ART OXFORD   ARTS COUNCIL ENGLAND   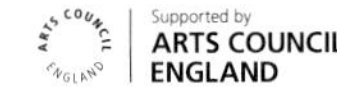 supported by   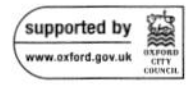 BUNDESKANZLERAMT ÖSTERREICH